Laura,

God's rich blessings to
You in your ministry!

Bill Oli

LEADING PEOPLE FROM THE MIDDLE

THE UNIVERSAL MISSION OF HEART AND MIND

William P. Robinson

Executive
Excellence
Publishing

For permission requests, contact the publisher at:

Executive Excellence Publishing
1366 East 1120 South
Provo, UT 84606
Phone: 1-801-375-4060
Toll Free: 1-800-304-9782
Fax: 1-801-377-5960
www.eep.com

For Executive Excellence books, magazines and other products, contact Executive Excellence directly. Call 1-800-304-9782, fax 1-801-377-5960, or visit our website at www.eep.com.

Printed in the United States

10 9 8 7 6 5 4 3 2 1

Library of Congress Cataloging-in-Publication Data

Robinson, William, 1949-
  Leading people from the middle / By William Robinson.
     p. cm.
Includes bibliographical references.
  ISBN 1-930771-25-8
 1. Leadership. 2. Middle managers. 3. Executive ability. 4. Communication in organizations. I. Title.
  HD57.7 .R635 2002
  658.4'3--dc21
                    2002004746

Advance Praise for
LEADING PEOPLE
FROM THE MIDDLE

Bill Robinson, an extraordinarily gifted leader of a flourishing college, offers vision and practical strategies for effective leadership. Moreover, he writes with wit and wisdom borne of his social science expertise and street-smartened experience, making this a quick and captivating read. For leaders facing 21st century challenges, *Leading People from the Middle* offers hope and direction.
—David Myers, Hope College, author of *Intuition: Its Powers and Perils*

A "must read" for executives in creative, fast-paced organizations. *Leading People from the Middle* does not imply weakness—just the opposite. In this extraordinarily thoughtful volume, Dr. William P. Robinson pieces together the best leadership lessons of the 20th Century with his sage views of the needs of the 21st Century. He shows how vision, goals, direction, analysis, and "opportunity seizing" can be combined with consensus building, decentralization, "influencing from among," and "living in the center of mission." In so doing, he crafts a unique style of paradoxical leadership which enables leaders to be "laid back and aggressive, strong and vulnerable, caring and cold blooded," depending upon the exigencies of situations and structures. Robinson has found a novel and implementable approach to leadership which allows leaders to be at once optimally adaptable, open to opportunities, and above all, connected to their stakeholders.
—Robert J. Spitzer, S.J., Ph.D., president, Gonzaga University

Leading People from the Middle accurately describes what happens on the Whitworth College campus under the leadership of Bill Robinson. It is very clear that Bill is called to be a leader. He is truly a leader from the middle—a consensus builder who is not afraid to make decisions. As you read his reflections, you have a very clear sense of him. He is genuine, generous, engaging, self-aware, and focused on the important issues and speaking the truth. The very best leadership is used to move an organization to a new position. Bill is into leadership for the exciting work, not the role.

When you're on Whitworth College campus, you see the wonderful camaraderie between Bill and the students. It is a very casual, but mutually respectful relationship. Bill is genuinely interested in them and their experience. Yet there is also no doubt about who the leader is. He teaches and leads these students by example—from the middle.

—Violet A. Boyer, president/CEO, WAICU/ICW

Leading People from the Middle is must reading for today's managers who want to be tomorrow's business leaders. Dr. Robinson, a skillful author and educator, combines academic integrity with a warm, personal style of writing to explain how the present-day style of management evolved and what it takes to become more effective in the current business environment.

—Charles L. Boppell, president and CEO, Worldwide Restaurant Concepts

Bill Robinson forces us to evaluate our own leadership styles in light of well-defined changes in 21st century organizational life. His informality and subtle humor make this an easy book to read, but you can't stop thinking about how you will solve the paradoxical demands on your role. He melds scholarship and experience well.

—Robert C. Andringa, Ph.D., president,
Council for Christian Colleges & Universities

As a leader, educator and author, Bill Robinson's greatest insights come from his everyday, never-ending, up-close-and-personal contact with people. This book's unique contribution is its grounding in the understanding of the needs and desires of people. Bill's leadership construct is people-based. Eschewing theories and formulas, this book offers principles that are derived from the needs and idiosyncrasies of those being led. No other approach will prove more practical for those leading in the increasingly paradoxical world of tomorrow. Read it—and you will never enjoy leading from behind a desk again!

—Richard J. Umbdenstock, president and CEO, Providence Services

ADVANCE PRAISE

Bill Robinson's vision of leadership comes from the right places—from his good heart, his deep belief in God, and his abiding faith in human nature. Those who share his vision will be free to be graceful and grateful leaders, prepared for the unexpected and excited for the opportunities that life and leadership present.

—George R. Nethercutt, Jr., representative in Congress

Simply writing about leadership is like finding guards for a basketball team—they are a dime a dozen. But when you find a guard that leads by word and action in all that he does, then you have found the diamond in the rough. Bill Robinson not only presents a great read, but he lives out the words in this book. I've witnessed first hand Bill's ability to lead within a community. As a former employee under Bill, I learned a great deal about leadership through watching and listening. The pages that follow are from a man who is talking the talk, and walking the walk.

—Steve Alford, head coach Iowa basketball

Bill Robinson alerts us to the serious changes taking place in the leader's job and raises the crucial question of the relationship of organizations and society. Good stuff!

—Max DePree, author of *Leadership Jazz*

For

Bonnie

Acknowledgements

For allowing me to work in their midst—the students, faculty, staff, trustees, and alumni of Whitworth College.

For their great help in this project—Sylvia Hedrick, Greg Orwig, Terry Mitchell, Jack Burns, Scott McQuilkin, Ken West, Em Griffin, Mark Jessen.

For leading me—John Thatcher, Chuck Boppell, Jim Singleton, John Young, Ed Butterbaugh, A. Blair Helman, Phil Clement, Glenn Heck, Orley Herron, John Huffman, Woody Strodel, Terry Pickett, Gordon Loux, Jack and Theo Robinson, Jim and Annette Carmean, Ed and Nancy Robinson, and most of all, Paul and Lillian Robinson—my first and best leaders.

For special support during this project—Lar, Pat, Dave, Ron, Ken, Steve, (and their great families), the president's cabinet, my Whitworth basketball friends (just the ones who pass me the ball), Rich, Don, Chris, Terry, Bob, Steve, and most of all, Tom Robinson.

For giving me Brenna, Ben and Bailley—the amazing grace of God.

Contents

Preface

The hardest part of writing this book was plugging my ears to an imaginary voice I heard every time I sat down to write. "Please," said the voice, "not another book on leadership." Actually, the voice wasn't imaginary; it was my voice. I'm weary of books on leadership. It's not that the publications are bad. In fact, many of them are very interesting and thought-provoking. But most of the leadership books I've read haven't really helped me become a better leader. That could be my fault—I don't give them much of a chance. Most of the books flunk my "Goldilocks" test in the first few chapters: "This book's too theoretical," "This book's too anecdotal," "Ah, this book is just right." Goldilocks had better luck with soup, chairs, and beds than she's likely to have with leadership books.

I'm not going to be shocked if this book also gets tossed onto the compost heap of leadership literature. It is neither a textbook nor a how-to manual, although it contains elements of both. *Leading People from the Middle* is the product of my reunion with leadership research that I once knew well, but have visited sporadically since becoming "a leader." In a readable fashion, I've presented theoretically sound principles and experientially proven ways to think about leading, not to mention a few suggestions for becoming better at it. Most of the ideas in this book have emerged from looking at theoretical models through the eyes of experience. I have discovered that my trek through 16 years as a college president gives a different look to the studies I "mastered" as a Ph.D. student in organizational communication.

Leading People From the Middle

My hope in writing this book is that its readers will become better at leading. "Well, of course," you say. You'd be surprised. Actually, the great works on leadership have sought to help readers understand leadership more than to improve their practice of the art.

Our most famous leadership titan, James MacGregor Burns, has written what some call the definitive work on leadership. In fact, it's so definitive that it bears the simple title *Leadership*.[1] Burns's *tour de force* offers an incredibly comprehensive theory of leadership, and someone with a fertile imagination could undoubtedly infer something applicable from his book for every leadership situation. But Burns sets forth his case from a very conceptual perspective.

I think of myself as a student-practitioner of leadership. I have not written as a scholar to enlighten other students of the field. I certainly do not present myself as an expert leader in hope of helping fine-tune other expert leaders. Fifteen years ago, a friend gave me a videotape by Jack Nicklaus entitled, "Golf My Way." "Ah," I thought, "these would be the tips I need to master this frustrating sport." My recollection is that the video began by presenting the best golfer in the universe explaining the game's technical, physiological, and mental intricacies. After teasing me for a while with talk about hips and shoulders, he stepped up to the tee and smacked the cover off the ball. He followed up his drive by slamming a monstrous seven-iron 180 yards to within 12 feet of the pin, and then rammed his birdie putt in the back of the cup. "Golf my way, folks," he beamed. I doubt if that's how it happened, but that's how I remember it. When I tried it his way, I wanted his result. I swung so hard they needed a backhoe to get me unscrewed out of the ground; so on the second shot I went back to my pathetic way. I'm afraid most books on leadership present either a Nicklaus standard or a James MacGregor Burns explanation. Both feel out of reach to me as I look for better ways to lead the college where I work.

So, I think I have an empathy advantage over most authors on leadership. I am not a leadership scholar, nor would anybody consider me the Jack Nicklaus of leadership, urging you to lead "my way." As I have suggested, much of what has been written on leadership takes the Nicklaus approach, providing anecdotal conclusions from the best leaders in the best companies, or the Burns method of citing studies by scholars who are seldom called upon to lead their organizations. Yet the question remains as to whether the readers of these success stories and theories become better leaders. Have we really looked at ways to take sound theory and transform it into working knowledge that can help make people more effective leaders? Too often the bridge to practice is left to be designed and constructed by the reader.

Having served this fine "whine" about leadership publications, I confess that people who begin books by knocking prior attempts come across as very arrogant to me (actually, I'm afraid anyone who writes a book on leadership probably suffers from an obese self-esteem). I find it especially offensive when we literary newcomers saunter into the foray with a look that says, "Relax kids, truth has arrived" on our faces. I don't feel that way, but I am not alone in my frustration about the helpfulness of leadership literature. Joseph Rost, a respected veteran scholar of this field, writes, "In other words, though practitioners read the leadership definitions of these scholars and study their models of leadership, they find it almost impossible to integrate and synthesize a clear, consistent picture of what leadership is and how leaders and followers actually engage in leadership."[2]

My Perspective

So why should my stuff be spared from the dreaded "interesting but not so helpful" review? First, leadership is central to both my discipline and my job. My field of study is the behavioral sciences, particularly organizational behavior. As a doctoral student, I began an earnest and enduring interest in leadership. Second, I have been a college president since 1986, and colleges present some especially difficult leadership challenges. Third, and probably what helps me most in understanding leadership, I've used my expertise in the behavioral sciences to understand my experiences as a college president. I think I've become a much more effective leader over the years. Both theoretically and practically I've learned how to engineer personal change. The reader will find "bridges" throughout this book. In the last section, I lay out a formula for really changing the way we lead.

LEADING PEOPLE FROM THE MIDDLE

Before I outline my approach to leadership, you need to be aware of several assumptions I make about leadership that, perhaps, contribute to the lack of orthodoxy in my principles and practices. These assumptions work their way into all of my observations, ideas and suggestions.

First, I can't golf Jack's way, and you can't lead my way. You wouldn't want to, and the people you lead wouldn't want you to either. Only I can lead my way, and sometimes it's pretty bizarre. According to our fund-raising consultant, I'm not very presidential. I consider this high praise. We have to work within our basic dispositions to be effective. After I smashed up the "My Way" golf video, my wife bought me a golf lesson from a human for my birthday. I knew I had the right guy when he said, "Look Doc, your shoulders and torso are smaller than Olive Oyl's, but you have Popeye's arms. We're going to build off that." We can dramatically improve the tools we have been given, but it doesn't work to try trading them in for a new set. My dad was a good mechanic. My mechanical abilities were sized up by my in-laws, who gave me a hammer with a pasted label on the handle that said, "Hammer: Use when you want to pound things." But one mechanical thing I did learn from my dad was, "Don't force it." You cannot be anything you want to be, no matter how hard you work at it. Motivational speakers, not to mention your dad, love telling you that you can be anything you want to be. They're lying. You can't. You can only use the tools in your kit. You can perfect them and even use them differently, but you have to be you. Leaders who force themselves to use an alien style or technique will not be effective.

Second, you can change. Personality theorist George Kelly observed, "We are neither prisoners of our history nor our heredity."[3] My job is to lead the process of transforming young people. I don't mean this in the James MacGregor Burns sense of transformation. I refer to what happens in the lives of college students during their years of living and studying with us at Whitworth College. Building on the personality and gifts they bring to campus, these students blend information, values, and practices into their lives, producing staggering changes. Change is not the exclusive property of the young. In several of Tom Peters' leadership books, he makes reference to Weaver Popcorn of Van Buren, Indiana. I know the Weaver family well. Their company is extraordinarily successful thanks to the leadership provided by Welcome Weaver, former president and board chair, and by his son, Mike Weaver, current president. I met Mike in 1986. He was a devoted fan of the "in-your-face" Indiana University basketball coach, Bob Knight; and a couple of his employees mentioned to me that it showed. Because of some deep personal and professional reflection, Mike decided to change the way he and the company would view the Weaver Popcorn employees. The change was authentic and penetrating. Both Mike and the company were transformed. Mike is still Mike, but he sees his world through a different lens. Welcome and his wife, Adah, still shake their heads in disbelief at Mike's change. It is my intention to provide the theory and application that can lead to a Mike Weaver-type change.

Third, there are moral absolutes. The gist of this book is taking what we have learned about leadership over the past 100 years and building the most useful concepts into a working repertoire. It will feel, as you read, as if the acid test of whether a concept is useful is whether it works. That tone could lead you to assume that I lay my sacrifices on the altar of pragmatism. Such is not the case. On issues with moral dimensions I have conditioned myself to look above the bottom line. My parents were models of this virtue, and on all things ethical, I still look up to my three older siblings who took the lead of our wonderful parents and have each accepted the call to gospel ministry. My moral absolutes find their origin in my Christian faith. I believe the Bible to be reliable and true. Since faith is the basis for these absolutes, I try to not be judgmental of those who find true north at a different point on their moral compasses. But I won't compromise on my north. I have left two jobs on ethical grounds (both times to better situations, lest you think I'm more noble than is the case).

In the pages that follow, I have attempted to highlight and apply important findings in this relatively new field of leadership. I have not, however, tried to suppress my own voice. It is through the eyes of my experience that I interpret theoretical concepts. To feign total objectivity is neither honest nor enjoyable in this kind of writing exercise. I hope readers will find both honesty and joy on every page.

My Definition of Leadership

To say the least, the definition of leadership is a moving target. A hundred years ago we just had leaders. "Leadership" hadn't even found its way into the dictionary until the late 1800s. When it did, "leadership" simply referred to the qualities and actions of a leader. Now, by some definitions, it doesn't matter whether you serve as the mayor or the village idiot, you can still provide leadership. This book will trace the 20th-century progression of how we think about leadership. But I'll warn you, we still haven't got it figured out very precisely.

I have a friend named Jack Burns. He's a professor and a scholar in the field of leadership. (Jack is refreshing because he knows the difference between being a scholar and being an expert. Many scholars consider themselves experts. I considered myself an expert on teenagers until I had three of my own ransacking our house. Most of the studies in Sections II-IV were conducted by "experts." One of the reasons why I once wanted to stop being a president and join a faculty was so that I could become an "expert" on leadership rather than one who actually had to provide it.) According to Jack, his field has not come up with a commonly accepted definition of leadership. It is amazing that an entire field of study can't even agree on what it is they're studying. As I mentioned in my introduction, Joseph Rost feels leadership scholars are in definitional disarray. In *Leadership for the 21st Century*, he reports that in examining 587 studies on leadership he found 221 definitions.[4] Apparently, the other 366 thought the definition to be self-evident. It's hard not to get the feeling that, similar to the beholders of beauty, leadership is in the eye of the led.

Jack Burns published a long article, "Defining Leadership: Can we see the forest for the trees?", in *The Journal of Leadership Studies*.[5] In the article he wove together the definitions of several leadership hotshots—notably James MacGregor Burns, Ronald Heifetz and Joseph Rost—in an attempt to find some kind of big picture of leadership. In general, Jack likes James MacGregor Burns's idea of leadership as the process of transforming the attitudes and behaviors of the group. This transformation requires both the leader and the followers to adapt themselves in order to accomplish the goal. Jack makes the case that "Leadership can be exercised by a person (or group) with an established role (e.g. the mayor or the village idiot) in an organization."

This evolved concept of leadership is not exactly the way Teddy Roosevelt thought about it when he was leading the Rough Riders up San Juan Hill at the beginning of the 20th century. During the last 100 years, the trend of leadership in America has moved steadily away from the person in charge. So can the person in charge still lead? Absolutely. But her or his position of leadership no longer finds itself exclusively in the front; rather, leadership is now exercised from a full 360-degree angle. That's why "leading from among" is where the leader wants to be.

My working definition of leadership is pretty simple. I define leadership as "extraordinary influence that finds its source in a person or group." First, we all exercise influence of some kind. If our influence is ordinary, that's life, not leadership. Second, extraordinary things happen that alter the flow of events. Leadership occurs when a person or group, rather than some external force, causes the extraordinary to happen. Does that mean Hitler meets my definition of a leader? Yes, but his brand of leadership screams for an adjective—"heinous" gets close. Any leadership theorist who builds virtue into his or her definition of leadership makes "bad leadership" an oxymoron; unless by "bad" one means "no leadership." Furthermore, defining leadership as necessarily good defies our normal vernacular. We often talk about ineffective leadership. I can't argue that my definition of leadership is the best one, but it's the one I assume in this book.

My Purpose

I have made no attempt to write "The Five Steps to Leading," or "Leadership Made Simple." I agree with H.L. Mencken, who said, "For every complex problem there's a simple answer, and it's wrong." Leading is not simple; but it can be done effectively by everyday people. I've written for those people, the ones who are responsible for helping groups in their efforts to accomplish important and challenging tasks.

I suppose this book will be most helpful to people who find themselves holding rather significant supervisory responsibilities, largely because that's my vantage point when I look at the leadership enterprise. I make the assumption that the reader occupies a position from which leadership is needed and expected. Having learned much from leaders outside my field, I think the ideas in this book will hold value beyond the world of education, even though that's my world.

I should also add that my observations will make more sense to the reluctant leader than to the ambitious one. My first performance review in my current position contained an interesting quote from a faculty member: "He loves Whitworth College more than he loves being its president." No higher compliment could have been bestowed upon me. I'm at Whitworth College because I absolutely love the place. I'm its president because "college president" is what I do (much more than who I am). I never planned to do this kind of work. I slipped into the role at a relatively young age, and I failed in several attempts to slip out. I was suckered into applying for the position when two of my demons, Overconfidence and The-Need-For-Attention, conspired with a personal restiveness about our living situation. After a few years, I considered returning to faculty life, but I discovered through a couple of instant rejections that not too many faculty clubs have revolving doors.

Sometimes I feel I'm on "the road I should not have taken." In my opinion, I'm a better teacher than president. And my dad was right: I don't particularly like responsibility. But my parents also instilled in me a sense of pride that makes me want to do what it takes to be the best president I am capable of being. Certainly, there are parts of the job I like very much. All I'm saying is that you'll find my ideas especially helpful if you've been cast into leadership rather than held it as a life-long dream. Maybe it's because I backed into this job that I feel no loyalty to the conventions of being a college president. In fact, I've often felt that anyone who aspires to be a college president is probably too stupid to do the job.

Introduction

I wish I had a grand metaphor for what I mean by "leading from the middle." It's too bad I don't picture a leader like that glorious goose in the front of the "V," leading its gaggle in formation to their destiny, interrupting century-old migratory patterns only to loiter on golf courses or make deposits on clean cars. But, alas, I don't. Another picture, I suppose, is a soccer game of four-year olds. Picture the lifeless ball as the leader, always in the middle of the pack, always getting kicked around by little people. Other than the ball being in the middle, that metaphor doesn't work either.

Over the course of this book, it will become clear that my understanding of leading from the middle refers to influencing from among, rather than from above, below, or in front of one's group. It refers to the non-aloof ways in which leaders should see themselves. Leading from the middle refers to positioning ourselves alongside those whom we've empowered. It refers to walking the regression line, equidistant from the poles we have to visit if we are to be effective leaders in the 21st century. Leading from the middle refers to living in the center of a mission, rather than simply lifting it up. Using a term from Christian theology, leading from the middle refers to leadership that "incarnates" the mission. The Christian story is that the method God chose to lead a fallen human race to redemption was by "[becoming] flesh and [dwelling] among us."[1]

I have found from studying the history of leadership, as well as from my own experiences, that leading from the middle is a very effective way for leaders to think about their styles and strategies. I am not saying that the coach-leader, the servant-leader, the charismatic-leader or the lofty-leader are ineffective models of leadership. What I am saying is that working from the middle puts the leader in the best place to develop and use effectively the best influence tools.

Five Sections

I have divided this material into five sections:

Section I: 21st Century Leadership. In the 21st century strong leaders will be back in favor, but the good ones will be different from their 20th century ancestors. They will stand in a different place and use a different set of skills. In this section, we will look at how large, small, and even tiny organizations will become more federated. This decentralization of power and sometimes geography will produce the need for paradoxical leadership. Consistency will be far less important than adaptability. Good leaders will spend most of their time in the middle of the action while sliding deftly back and forth between polar opposites in style. They will be laid-back and aggressive, strong and vulnerable, caring and cold-blooded. They will know the paradoxes of their positions and navigate them well. The 21st century leaders will also develop other qualities—some because of the federated structures of their organizations and others because of societal needs.

Sections II–IV: Lessons from 20th-Century Approaches to Leadership. Section II–IV explore earlier iterations of today's most effective leadership models and qualities. In so doing, these sections trace an interesting trend in leadership over the past 100 years. In the early part of the century, leadership was thought to be found rooted in the personality traits of those who were chosen to lead—leaders were born, not made. By the 1970s, leadership had inched so far away from the personality of the leader that leaderless leadership had become the rage. The leader was defined as anyone in the group who performed acts of leadership. The 20th century systematically decentralized leadership away from the office of the leader by spreading it across the organization. This decentralization of leadership should shock no one. During that same period organizations moved from very centralized and hierarchical structures to more decentralized, flatter models. It is speculative to argue whether one was the cause or effect of the other, but in the history of business the 20th century will go down as one of decentralization.

Section II, III, and IV trace this history of leadership through three overlapping stages without assuming, as do many leadership theorists, that each stage corrects the errors of periods gone by. A great deal can be learned by discussing the most seminal and enduring findings from each of the three eras.

Section V: Changing the Way We Lead. Without a doubt, the most frequently asked question in the field of leadership is some variation on the issue of whether leaders are born or made. In Section V I put on my behavioral scientist hat and argue that they can be made. People can and do change. In the 1970s a couple of researchers at the University of Illinois, Fishbein and Ajzen, set out to explain why attitude change was so unpredictable.[2] Their findings led to what I believe are the basic components of behavior. I cast these components as steps for changing our behavior. These steps work whether we're trying to change the manner in which we treat subordinates or trying to change our diet. In fact, people who go through dramatic behavioral change go through these steps, whether they know it or not.

Reflections. From 1996 through 1999 I managed to squeeze two study weeks into the summers. Each exquisite day I read, wrote, and thought about life and work while sitting at our getaway cabin on the Pend Oreille River. Occasionally I recorded my reflections on what I had been learning. Without my necessarily intending it, these thoughts took the form of leadership lessons. Because many of these reflections seemed relevant, I have tucked them into discussions throughout the book.

Section I
21st Century Leadership

In the summer of 2000, we sent our kids—ages 22, 19, and 16—to Europe for a summer. One night I received a call from them informing me that they had left Budapest so that they could arrive in Prague early the next morning, which, apparently, is the best time to get into a youth hostel or one of the "no-star" hotels that they became masters at finding. For a month they finessed their way across Southern and Eastern Europe, communicating with us daily through whatever technological device was cheapest. Working the technology system is like riding a bike for these kids. During their trip I ran into a high school senior who said, "Hey Bill, I got a call on my cell phone while I was shopping yesterday. It was Ben, calling from Barcelona." No big deal at only 17 cents per minute. Managing the cultures didn't pose too many problems for our young travelers either. They are sensitive and fearless. Borders, boundaries and distance function as details of minor consequence for their generation.

So, why did we send our kids to Europe with only Eurorail passes, a very loose itinerary, and one rule—communicate with us somehow everyday? Because if these three young people hope to do anything more than eek by in the 21st century, they better be able to navigate both technology and the globe. They are citizens of a very different world than the 20th century world that their parents understand. In *The Lexus and the Nexus,* Thomas Friedman says it best, "The world is 10 years old. Globalization and technology have created a new world."

Organizations big and small in the early part of this century will differ in many ways from their ancestors, but I suspect no changes will rival the magnitude of impact caused by globalization and technology. Leadership needs will inevitably undergo changes as direct and indirect forces of globalization and technology bend the old organizational rules. This claim is not exactly a news flash, but not everyone knows how to respond. As a rule, you can get kicked just as hard by overreacting to technology changes as you can by lingering behind the rear-end of the status quo donkey. I heard about a university library that 20 years ago crowned microfiche as the technology of the 21st century, then dropped several million on a massive conversion. Oops.

In formulating my ideas about the next wave of leadership, I have attempted to identify the type of leadership needed to meet the demands created by technology, globalization and other contemporary organizational trends. Because 20th century studies revealed many durable insights about leadership—ones that still apply today—the focus of this first section is on leadership needs that differ from those emphasized in the 20th century. I suspect leaders have always benefited from the characteristics being called out by today's organizations, but the new world makes necessities out of what might have been considered luxury qualities in the past.

Scholars in the 20th century may not have unearthed all the answers about leadership, but they did raise a fundamental three-part question that still points us in a very enlightening direction: "What are the traits, styles, and cultural influences that leaders need to provide?" In this section I have suggested 21st century answers to those three questions. Although I find moderation rather boring, I have tried to avoid the extremes of being too hip about the future or too romantic about the past. No one can foretell the magnitude of change that awaits organizational life, but the trends seem clear and the most effective leaders will get out in front of them.

Exhorting leaders to march out in front of 21st century organizational trends begs the question of what 21st century leadership will really look like. In 1991 Joseph Rost published a book entitled *Leadership for the Twenty-First Century*. Among his many points, two jump off of every page. First, we don't have an agreed-upon or adequate definition of "leadership." Second, what we do have suffers from the anachronistic assumptions of an industrial paradigm. Rost's insightful, if occasionally whiny, critique concludes by calling for a post-industrial paradigm. Unfortunately, Rost doesn't detail exactly what the post-industrial paradigm looks like. He does, however, deliver a post-industrial definition of leadership. Leadership, for Rost, is "an influence relationship among leaders and followers who intend real changes that reflect their mutual purposes." Rost defends the post-industrial nature of his definition in claiming, "this paradigm shift is massive and is immediately evident from the complete separation of leadership from management inherent in the definition."[1] Separating leadership from management isn't exactly a new thought. Warren Bennis had already been making a living off broadcasting this distinction for 15 years. What I suspect Rost considers unique about his differentiation is the insistence that leadership deploys a collaborative model for mutual benefit, not simply for improved performance. Bennis and others, not quite as noble as Rost, encourage collaboration between leaders and their groups primarily in the name of increased productivity.

I cite Rost as prologue to a couple disclaimers. First, I'm still looking for details about that post-industrial paradigm. I can be convinced to bid farewell to industrial society, but I know that we still have to make stuff. Not everybody can sell insurance or be a webmaster. It remains to be seen if Rost's post-industrial leadership ideas will work all that well a half-mile down my street at Kaiser Aluminum, or at any other manufacturing enterprises. His point that the 21st century trends lean toward collaboration and away from rigid hierarchies is one with which I very much agree. I'm just not sure the trends floating around in my crystal ball meet the criteria of this "massive paradigm shift." Second, I agree that leadership and management are two quite different activities. But I rather dislike leadership theorists' condescending tones when they spell out its difference from management. In everyday life, leaders without management savvy or skills will discover their leadership house is built on sand. Good management comes less easily to me than leadership. I know this, and the people who report to me know this. When I get sloppy on agendas, individual meetings, performance reviews, and other routine management activities, the people who report to me lose direction and my big picture gets blurred. I can't lead well without managing adequately.

Essential 21st Century Leadership Qualities

I have identified six qualities that I believe will empower the person who leads any organization through the first part of this century. The six qualities taken together blend to include traits, styles and influences—the three different ways to look at leadership provided us by 20th-century approaches. Strength in only one of those ways—the right traits, the right style or the right transforming influence—will fall short of meeting the leadership demands of the new century. The most effective leaders will integrate qualities in a way that blurs the 20th century distinctions. They will be people whose impact results from the synergy of blended qualities.

The most effective leadership in the new century will be:

• *Paradoxical:* The nimble leader who knows when to tote the lunch pail and when to lift the sceptre, the leader who moves humbly among all people until it is time to step forward with unshakeable confidence, rallying the people with a simple, "Let's roll."

• *Secure:* Leaders who delight so much in the accomplishments of others that they barely notice their own inestimable role in the success; leaders whose selflessness energizes all those around them.

• *Communicative:* Leaders who realize that silence is more deadly than golden, that good decisions come from good information, and that "no information" speaks volumes.

• *Inspiring:* Leaders who find their way to the sanctuary of our souls; leaders who can knit heart and mind into a compelling mandate.

• *Virtuous:* Leaders whose uncompromising goodness quietly beckons the most valuable gift that any follower gives to any leader—trust.

• *Driven and rhythmic:* Leaders with the capacity to find their highest productivity groove, the flow of life and work in which currents work together toward personal and professional fulfillment.

In suggesting these qualities, I am assuming that leaders possess: sufficient intelligence, sufficient expertise in the task or enterprise that they are leading, and a commitment to continuous learning. These three characteristics are fundamental to any leadership effort. Without them, leadership will always be misguided.

Chapter 1
21st Century Trends

Prophesying general directions for new-century organizations poses less of a challenge than figuring out specific destinations. Only omniscient 26-year-old Wall Street analysts think they can intuit the exact specifications of the typical 2020 organization. But the early 21st century does reveal some pretty clear trends. Most organization trends evolve in the private sector, get copied by the not-for-profits, are forced upon public enterprises, and eventually show up in non-formal affiliation groups. Generally, these trends undergo contextualizing of some kind in order to make them fit the situations, but they still push their way into an outfit's operations or culture. For example, the service rage of the 1980s, displayed by companies such as Nordstrom and Scandinavian Airline Systems, invaded hospitals, schools, government, and every other customer-dependent line of work (except toll booths). So the trends we see in the business organization will, ultimately, affect all organizations in some form.

Characteristics of 21st Century Organizations

I see many fads and directions in today's organizations, but three solid trends seem like sure-bets to last well into the 21st century. These characteristics are neither new nor exclusive properties of this era. They are simply organizational traits that we will see with greater frequency and magnitude. I believe businesses will become more: federated, adaptive, and connected.

LEADING PEOPLE FROM THE MIDDLE

1. Federated. Last month I enjoyed a dinner in Seattle with a friend of mine who worked for three different companies—Ma Bell, Ameritech and Southern Bell—all without leaving his employer. Having lived through the government breakup of Ma Bell, and the SBC takeover of Ameritech, this 40-something man now had the responsibility of setting up a business for SBC in Seattle. After peppering him with questions, I concluded that the principal resources this new business would receive from the parent company were start-up capital and organizational culture. Certainly, the company brand would serve well in this venture, but for the most part, my buddy was building a business that would learn from the parent company, and then stand on its own.

It is possible that becoming federated, more than the other two trends, correlates with the size of an organization. But even small organizations will locate responsibility and authority farther from the center and closer to their dispersed customer bases than they once did. During my graduate studies I conducted a few research projects in network analysis (back then, "network" enjoyed the stable life of a noun. Now it races around trading business cards and kissing fannies in its frenetic life as a verb). Because my primary interest focused on the conditions under which centralized and decentralized networks prove most effective, I have always looked at organizations on this continuum. But "federated" provides a more apt description of this trend than "decentralized." Charles Handy penned a wonderful chapter on federated organizations in his book, *Beyond Certainty.*[1] He helps explain the difference.

Handy points out that in most decentralized organizations, the center usually delegates jobs, responsibility and even authority to the outer units. In a federated organization, the center provides only what the units can't effectively provide for themselves. It is like the states granting powers to the federal government, rather than the other way around. A balance of power exists as both the cause and the effect of many centers throughout the federation. Handy notes that the corporate center exists to coordinate, not to control.[2] For this reason, he argues that federalist centers should always be small, if not minimalist. Federations are held together by trust, interdependence and common goals. Group members hold dual citizenship in both the subsidiary and the federation.

In the 21st century, globalization will make federations desirable, while technology will make them possible. Staying involved with a geographically dispersed customer base will not stand in the way of close communication and feedback within the federation. Technology will allow workers to be in touch with each other while being "out there" with customers. Furthermore, employees' proximity and engagement with the constituencies they serve will turn orders from headquarters into the famous last words of companies who don't listen to the folks on the front lines. I should also mention that organizational federalism will surface not only in the sprawling multinational corporations, but even in small groups. Wherever we find independent group members or units, held together by a mutual need rather than structural cords, we find a federated environment. This authentic distribution of rights and responsibilities alters irreversibly the relationship between the leader and the led. Central powers become more limited and the roles of the leader become ones of coordinator, strategist, resource broker, vision builder, motivator and encourager.

Perhaps federalism will prove to be the basic organizational model of the 21st century, maybe even Rost's post-industrial paradigm. For that to happen, more than structures will have to change. Warren Bennis comments, "The most practical solution, particularly for large corporations, is federalism. Federations work better than monolithic organizations because, along with strength, they offer flexibility. They are more nimble and adaptive. They have all the inherent advantages of being big but all the benefits of being small."[3]

Federalist thinking must replace the policy-driven, hierarchical patterns of thinking. "Follower" questions, such as "What would the center want me to do?" get shoved aside by "What is the best thing to do?" I think that day is upon us. In political history, federalism usually comes about by revolution. Textbooks aren't exactly littered with examples of voluntary federalism, as Handy points out. But globalization, technology, corporate mergers, fluid and disperse markets, and the demand on organizations to be both grand and personal could be the revolutionaries at the gate.

Former IBM chief, Lou Gerstner, observes, "The real revolution isn't about the technology itself. The real revolution here has to do with institutional change—the fundamental transformation of time-honored ways of doing things."[4]

2. Adaptive. Last summer my son and I built a computer, needless to say, it was a "virtual computer." Imagine a couple of technological boneheads slapping together a state-of-the-art laptop in about 45 minutes. In all probability, no other computer in the world bears exactly the same features and specifications as the one we built. When we finished, we conferred genius status on each other, and still had enough energy to go outside for a game of WWF one-on-one basketball. Four days later, our creation arrived at the door. The chefs at Dell had cooked up exactly what we had ordered.

Organizations that proudly decree, "What worked in the past will work in the future" can look forward to going under with their heads held high. Markets change and markets rule. Let's look at the computer example. I bought my first computer in 1981 after going to Sears and looking at their line. All I really needed was word processing and an electronic spreadsheet, but my choices were restricted, so my shiny, new Osborne had far more bells and whistles than I wanted. When my son Ben reached the point of buying a computer to take to college, he called the school's academic technologist and got the "must-have" list. After determining he wanted a laptop from Dell, he entered their website and made 32 decisions about features, with a running tab that calculated the cost of each choice (he owes me a lot of money). The company without the capacity to deliver exactly what Ben needed had better find lots of people my age who trust the manufacturer to guess right about what we need.

The last decade of the 20th century will be remembered as the point in history when the emergence of technology and the proliferation of market economies joined forces to change the world. Adaptation is the only way organizations can harness, even survive, the combustion of these two forces. Every day more people are demanding and getting what they want right now. All organizations, not just businesses, feel the effects of immediacy bearing down on them. When I was a boy, all the Presbyterians in Itasca, Illinois, went to the Itasca Presbyterian Church. Why wouldn't they? Maybe because consumerism had not yet become a sacrament. Now they go wherever they can best get what they want. Is this bad? Not necessarily, but it does change the rules.

It will be interesting to see if our sacred cows see the need to adapt. Not long ago I had to go to a meeting in Washington D.C. I discovered that I could buy a United Airlines round trip ticket to a D.C. airport for $1,710 or to Baltimore for $318. I also found out that the Baltimore flight would get me back to Spokane too late for a speech I had to give. I called the United number that we high mileage, prized customers use. I was delighted to find out that a flight from Reagan National in D.C. was half full and fit my schedule perfectly. So, I explained that I worked at a college and could not justify $1,710 dollars to go to a meeting, but I'd be willing to pay $750 to sit in one of those empty seats out of Reagan, otherwise I'd have to cancel the trip. "I'm sorry, I can't do that," she replied. "So you're going to throw away $750 minus the cost of my snack?" I asked. "I'm sorry there is nothing I can do," she helplessly replied. I didn't make the trip.

Even in running a business that trades on the tradition-rich value of the liberal arts, I deal daily with the need to make market and technology driven decisions. In 1986 I entered the college presidency believing that no student came to a small college out of affection for bureaucracy. I harped incessantly on the importance of being personalized in our treatment of students. In the first decade of the 21st century, providing personal attention isn't enough. We need to move from personalized service to individualized service, and there's a difference between the two. When Ben went out to test-drive computers, all the service stores gave him personal attention—treated him like a king, actually. But when it was time to slam down the money, he demanded a product customized for his individual needs more than he demanded love and attention. In this new century, organizations like Whitworth will inventory every service and every operation asking two questions: "Is this a point at which our mission will benefit from individualization?" and, "Does technology provide a means to individualize?" The personal adjustment serves as one example of the many adaptation demands that markets and technology will place on organizations.

The organization functions as a battleground for clashes between two primal human forces: resistance to change and pressure to adapt. Environmental systems work relentlessly to mold and shape us, like rushing water carves out canyons and attacks dams. Our internal defense systems fight valiantly to protect habits, predispositions and comfort zones from all the offensives launched by our environments. As an ordered collection of individuals, the organization becomes a macrocosm of this basic conflict between internal and external forces. With few exceptions, organizations find themselves in a Darwinian world that requires adaptation as a ticket for survival. Fortunately, this requirement often pays generous dividends. The sagacious Peter Drucker observes, "All great change in business has come from outside the firm, not from inside."[5] In this century, organizations will adapt. The question is not whether, but how?

3. Connected. Few people need to be convinced that the organizations of tomorrow will reach extraordinary levels of connectivity. The web of connections promises to move in all directions. Business organizations will expand connections with employees, customers, parent companies, research firms, and consultants. Non-business organizations will also erect internal and external networks to provide members with helpful ties.

Technology has eliminated all of our excuses for not communicating. Once we received a phone bill with what we believed were inaccurate charges. When I spoke with the phone company representative, he explained that the service we purchased didn't include certain types of operator-assisted phone calls. I maintained composure until he grunted, "You should have known…." "Scott," I responded, "I'm your customer. Your representative left out information in selling me a service. There's no excuse for that. You could have e-mailed me, faxed me, called me, or read me the terms. You had many options, but saying 'You should have known' is not one of those options. You will lose my business and I will be an eloquent critic of your company if these charges are not removed." Contrast this experience with a drugstore order I made over the Internet. After I filled my basket and clicked "Purchase," I heard that guy inside my e-mail system say, "You've got mail." The e-mail listed my items and provided a link I could click on if there were any errors in the order. And, in fact, I changed the order after changing my mind.

Because organizations will reach such high levels of connection, much of their success will depend on how well they maintain their networks. Overuse, underuse, and misuse pose equal threats. The old Marshall McLuhan aphorism that "the medium is the message" may be hyperbole, but it makes a pretty good point. Our abounding connections could use a few good masseuses to keep them supple and in good working order. The "when," "how," and "which" connection questions become vital in environments of virtually unrestricted information flow. In my work group, the president's cabinet, we chose to proscribe criticisms of each other by e-mail. It's too easy to fall into the trap of "If you can't say something nice, send it by e-mail."

Connection is in and distance is out. The organization of the 21st century had better know how to deal with that reality.

Two Other Trends

Most organizational theorists could round up a half-dozen or more 21st century trends that fall into the "obvious" category. My "Big Three"—Federated, Adaptive, and Connected—seem drop-dead certain to me, but I've included them because of the direct impact they have on leadership. The two characteristics listed below will likely be smaller waves to hit the organization beach. I suspect they will exercise a less-direct influence on the formula for successful leadership, but they will create a different atmosphere in our organizations.

Pedagogical. Korn-Ferry reports a sharp rise in the number of "chief learning officers" they're being asked to find. These folks scan their organizations for knowledge gaps, and then plug them with the abundant knowledge and information that they track externally. The current term we keep hearing from hotshot high-priced business consultants is "the learning organization." It may take some time to determine what this term actually means, but clearly organizations failing to tap into the knowledge explosion are tomorrow's dropouts.

Consummatory. Social seismologists find our most venerated institutions on shaky ground. The stability of marriage, family, church and even the Moose Lodge is being attacked by alternative choices. Although people have seemed willing to declare bank-ruptcy on their souls, they're less enthusiastic about losing their property (Machiavelli is getting smarter with each century). This trend, I believe, has created a cavernous spiritual vacuum. What else can explain the torrents of interest that have nudged spiritual-ity beyond serious business to big business? As our inner longings deepen, people's desire for the workplace to be more than a source of income will grow. They will seek meaning and fulfillment from the organization that employs them and from the voluntary groups they join. Membership will occur not simply for instrumental rea-sons, but also for consummatory aims.

The Big Question Mark

At the heart of the leadership challenge there lies a fundamen-tal question about the 21st century organization that goes beyond leadership: Will organizations return to being servants of their peo-ple, or will people continue to serve their organizations? Every organization ever formed began as a tool for people to accomplish something. Some person, or collection of persons, felt forming an organization would enable them to do more than what could be done by individuals. The organization served those who formed it as an instrument for achieving a common purpose. But somehow, for some reason, over some period of time, most organizations take on a life of their own, and the people become the servants of the orga-nizations. I'm not sure whether this inversion is a good or bad thing. While some have welcomed the stability of "serving the organiza-tion," others have battled the intransigence of companies that have institutionalized "the way our company does business." To date, nobody seems to have figured out how to reinvent mature organiza-tions on a monthly, quarterly or yearly basis, so it is not surprising that most big businesses have held their people in servitude.

In the 21st century we will have the tools to return organiza-tions to their early roles as servants. Will we run our organizations, or will our organizations run us? I suspect leaders of all organiza-tions will face the challenge of whether and how to take on this question. It is the cosmic question of change. It is the question of who owns whom.

Chapter 2
Paradoxical Leadership

Iknow a guy who almost became just the right leader. He's an uncompromising fellow, and for that I commend him. He bellied up to a nasty situation and took a lot of shots as he exposed wrongdoings. I admired him for his courage. I've been a dartboard on occasion myself, and it's no fun. Unfortunately, this person's leadership drive crashed after failing to negotiate a turn. He had gotten into a complex situation that required paradoxical leadership—any lasting solution would be the product of both a steely eye and a conciliatory spirit. There were enough missteps for everybody to join in the guilt. The torchbearer would have to lead back and forth between firm standards and generous forgiveness. This would-be leader did fine on the steely eye and firm standards part, but he couldn't bring himself to stop scolding the folks he considered the transgressors. He couldn't deal with the paradoxical need both to raze and raise.

Today's leaders must navigate the paradoxes inherent in the new organizational structures. The tall and tight hierarchies of years gone by tolerated less nimble leadership than will the federated enterprises of the 21st century. In a federation, the situation above could very easily occur when separate units angle their way into cross-purposes. No hope for mediation rests with the leader who shows up and delivers Rodney King's "Can't we just get along?" line; neither will the Wyatt Earp approach reconstruct productive relationships. The savvy leader will need to unearth the tension points and then traverse the paradoxical demands needed to renew productivity.

Wherever people or units have been empowered, even in small organizations, complexity results in the relationships between the whole and the parts, between the leader and the led. A sense of dual authority replaces the more orderly chain of command. This complexity creates the need for adaptive leadership that often touches opposite poles, depending on the nuances of the situation.

The Presidential Paradox

Where do we look for enlightenment on paradoxical leadership for today's federated organizations? At the risk of brash nationalism, I would suggest that a good place to start is perhaps the greatest federation in world history, The United States of America. The framers of the Constitution set up a leadership system characterized by limited powers, especially in the president's office. Article I stands guard against the strong-willed dictator, while Article II provides opportunities to wield forceful informal power, along with the formal powers placed under check. Clearly, the Constitution established the presidency as a job for the persuasive navigator. Congress would squash the monarch and the people would throw out the weakling. With unparalleled genius, Paine, Franklin, Madison, Hamilton and Jefferson led in the creation of a government with fluid, decentralized power. This may have been the first moment in history when one's leadership became more powerful than one's position as the leader.

I have a friend, Tom Cronin, who is a wonderful college president and one of the world's foremost authorities on the American presidency. He and Michael Genovese literally wrote the book on *The Paradoxes of the American Presidency*.[1] This engaging book, more than any other, has helped me understand the challenges of 21st century leadership. I find it absolutely fascinating that the U.S. Presidency offers a better laboratory now for understanding contemporary leadership than at any time in the past two centuries.

Tom and his co-author suggest nine paradoxes of the presidency. Four of the paradoxes that these authors find in the American presidency ring prophetic of the conflicting demands that most organizations will place on 21st century leadership. I have also presented an additional paradox leaders will face. Not to belabor the point, but when leaders authentically empower people or sub-units, they spread authority and limit their direct influence. By definition, this distribution creates paradoxical relationships. If leadership theorists agree on anything, it is the rising demand on leaders to empower those whom they lead. Real empowerment is not simply delegation; in fact, it is almost the opposite of what we sometimes think of delegation. When one is given a task by the leader to be done for the leader we're talking about a favor, not empowerment. Real empowerment results in high levels of independence and responsibility, and leading a group of empowered people can get complicated.

In the early decades of this century, leaders will create structures and relationships that federate power. These leaders cannot rely on the old ways of leading, unless, of course, they reach way back to the 200-year-old ways of leading nestled in the Articles of the United States Constitution.

Five Paradoxes

Of the five paradoxes below, the first four are of the United States Presidency.[2] These will find parallels in the leadership needed for today's organizations:

Paradox 1: Americans demand powerful, popular presidential leadership that solves the nation's problems; yet they are suspicious of strong, centralized leadership.

For seven years, I found myself in the vortex of this paradox. Manchester College is affiliated with the Church of the Brethren, one of America's four historic peace churches. Serving seven years as its president, I discovered a clear, and sometimes painful, perspective on the Church of the Brethren's historical suspicion of authority. At once it admired and feared strong leaders. This became clear to me when I noticed an ominous pattern. Current leaders were held in suspicion, former leaders were appreciated, and dead former leaders were venerated. Before making this observation, I felt the Brethren simply didn't happen to like any of the people in leadership. After my realization, I softened a bit, thinking maybe this peace church just enjoyed a non-ballistic form of target practice. Finally, I concluded that they really wanted centralized leadership, but feared centralized power. My effectiveness in this environment required both muscle and deference, and timing was everything. In an utterly implicit and unintentional way, the Church of the Brethren taught me the difference between the use of leadership and authority.

I feel the best way for leaders to manage this paradox is by using formal power as sparingly as possible, but "not never." In any group or organization, once the power decentralization occurs, any sign of retraction threatens the empowered. Leaders can learn from the American system of federal government and informally grant or formally structure a system of checks and balances. I find it helpful to think of my "formal power" as exhaustible credit, and to consider my informal influence as a means of replenishing tolerance for the times I need to use a formal, presidential chit. Using the very efficient and readily available power of my authority when I could engage people informally to support a similar or improved outcome, sneers at the benefits of federalism. I use a credit unnecessarily if not detrimentally. When I take the route of building consensus on an issue, I am nourishing the general confidence people have in my perspective, thus strengthening the base of my influence.

The paradox surfaces when we recognize that occasions do arise in which leaders must not be fearful of exercising authority over the decisions for which they will be held accountable. If we avoid those situations when formal power offers the only option to do what we believe is best for the organization, our informal influence erodes. A perception of weakness settles over our leadership. Judiciously "pulling rank" when the situation calls for it can strengthen leadership.

Using muscle always involves risk. Group members often chant, "Stronger, stronger . . . too strong!" It takes a pretty good shot to hit that narrow space between people's desire for "stronger" and their complaint of "too strong!" Sometimes people protest out of benign ignorance. After the Whitworth board of trustees delivered one of the few decisions that lies appropriately within a board's domain of decision-making, a faculty member crossly asked me, "How can they get away with that?" I didn't even understand the question. They're the trustees—that's what they do.

Authoritarian mandates that require cooperation raise the risk even higher, and the mandates had better work. "Lincoln is often criticized for acting outside the limits of the Constitution, but at the same time he is forgiven due to the obvious necessity for him to violate certain constitutional principles in order to preserve the Union."[3] I'm not sure the forgiveness would have been quite so generous had his efforts failed.

Leaders in this new century must be authoritative without being authoritarian. They must be forceful without forcing. The 20th century deal was that leaders would give power in exchange for productivity and fulfillment from those being led. Leaders can't take that power back. They must lead strongly, but with the sparing use of power. St. Paul captures the paradox in explaining that we need to be "unknown, yet well-known…sorrowful, yet rejoicing; poor, yet making many rich; having nothing, yet possessing all things…for when I am weak, then I am strong."[4]

Paradox 2: Americans yearn for the common person and also for the heroic, visionary performance.

I remember vividly when Tom Jarman, a close friend whom I lured from Northwestern University to become the Manchester College athletic director and wrestling coach, introduced me to his best friend, Denny. These two guys had wrestled on the same team in college, with Denny going into high school coaching and Tom coaching in the college ranks. Denny came across immediately as a regular guy, a fun-loving, old jock whom I felt I'd known for years. Now, Congressman Denny Hastert is two heartbeats away from the United States Presidency, serving his country as Speaker of the House of Representatives. I'm thrilled that "one of us" occupies this lofty office. Only in America…. On the other hand, I'm terrified that "one of us" is running Congress. What happens if an important vote comes before the House during a crucial World Series game? I have this admittedly fanciful and outdated image of Denny sitting up there in front of the U.S. House of Representatives with a transistor radio at his ear. As he peers over a large salad bowl overflowing with popcorn and pushes aside a couple of dead soldiers, Denny inadvertently changes the course of history when he pounds his gavel in delight over a "walk-off walk" in the 10th inning.

The Economist tells the story of a watering hole in Baltimore where a group of regulars were toasting the basic (and sometimes "base") views of Vice President Spiro Agnew. After their sudsy conferral of sainthood on Spiro, a journalist stunned the group by interrupting the coronation with the question of whether they'd like their man Spiro to be president. One bloke's reply illustrates the "commoner-king" paradox. "I don't want the president of the United States to sound like I do after a couple of beers," he said.[5] How does today's leader satisfy Americans' desire for leaders who are, in the words of Cronin and Genovese, "greater than anyone else, yet not better than themselves?"

My answer to this question is painfully trite, but painfully true. Today's leaders must come to terms with their own vulnerability. Often we talk about being vulnerable as an act of stooping, and a quite noble one for those leaders whose sweat doesn't smell bad. I can't stand it when leaders or speakers make a big deal about how they're going to be vulnerable and disclose some frailty. "Hey, leader, we never thought you were perfect; are you the last to know, or what?" The "King" side of the commoner-king paradox generally gets conferred upon leaders by virtue of their positions and skill sets. On the other hand, being a member of the "Commoner Club" requires an honest and open recognition that in so many areas we are vulnerable—just one stumble away from abject failure.

My best example of serving as commoner-king comes from a leadership position that gets smoked daily by this paradox: the cleric. My former pastor, Jim Singleton, is one of the most godly and human people I have ever met. By virtue of geography, our church represents a blend of professional and non-professional workers. When Jim left our church, we were all heartbroken because, to a person, we felt we were losing "one of us." Jim was our commoner because he knew, and we knew that he knew, that he just happened to be the "wretch like me" up front, using his rare gift for helping us grasp the impenetrable mysteries of a holy God. He was our king because his longing to know God gave honesty, elo-

Paradoxical Leadership

quence, and even royalty to the ordinary. As he met the ups and downs of life, he was just like us, but somehow better, and we loved having him as our leader.

Paradox 3: Americans want a just and compassionate President, yet they admire a cunning and, at times, ruthless leader.

The 21st century leader will need to move deftly between tender-heartedness and cold-bloodedness. In thinking about this paradox, it's hard not to conjure up images of the twisted morality that has "the godfather" roughhousing with his children in the morning and roughing up a "slow learner" in the afternoon. Actually, this paradox will unfold in quite the opposite manner in today's leadership. Leaders will need the ice in their veins on matters of principle and morality, but understanding hearts in their human relations. They must ruthlessly guard personal and organizational integrity, but that resolve must be carried out with justice and compassion.

Operating at only one pole on this paradoxical continuum won't work in the future, and wasn't effective in the past. In the early 1990s, Middlebury College in Vermont had a mess on its hands. Evidently, their operating budget turned red, so they hired a consulting firm to help trim their payroll. They made the cold-blooded decisions that needed to be made if they were to preserve the strength and integrity of the college. Unfortunately, the consultants were equally cold-blooded in executing (no pun intended) their conclusions. Pink slips and "Clear out your desk by noon tomorrow" notes violated the culture and the individual loyalty that characterized Middlebury. The consultants knew they'd made a mistake when faculty and staff arrived at commencement exercises in funeral regalia.

I've never made a really hard decision in which the victims cheered for me. But in those difficult moments of making the hard call, for some reason I felt a strong sense of compassion. I've felt this as both a leader, and a father. I recall one night when I delivered a totally arbitrary "no" to our 17-year-old son's request to join his friends in an inherently harmless activity, but one that I could not bring myself to approve. With tears streaming down his face, he blamed my decision on everything from me not trusting him to my

41

need to protect my own image. Fortunately, I didn't have it in me to accept his invitation to do battle. I was too sad about what it meant to fulfill my obligation as his father. I learned a good leadership lesson that night. Because of my commitment to my son's best interests, I could not compromise this decision, nor could it matter how cruel my authoritarianism felt to him. Precisely because it was my son I was facing, I ached horribly for the pain being endured by the boy who means more to me than any other male on this earth. And precisely because I was his dad, he recognized how much I hated the role of parent at that moment. By the end of the night, we were laughing at the naked shamelessness with which he had tried to leverage my guilt into some kind of payoff that I have now forgotten.

That night I went to bed thankful that I'd said no with a hanging head, rather than a stiff neck. Neither the hard-heartedness of my decision nor the soft-heartedness of my response could have survived that encounter without the primal love of the parent-child relationship. The clear lesson of the episode was my need to consider this paradoxical integration of opposites whenever I appear in front of the most difficult of decisions. Cold-blooded doesn't necessarily mean "arbitrary," but it does mean "difficult." I can't back down from that. Tender-hearted doesn't necessarily mean soft or even generous, but it always means compassionate and respectful. I violate everything I stand for if I protect myself with a cold veneer. Today's leaders must develop square jaws and soft hearts, and most importantly, must know when to lead with which.

I am aware that the paradox of compassionate and cold-blooded is not the same as compassionate and cunning. Cronin and Genovese found that American people believe that their President should, under some circumstances, resort to craft and guile in pursuit of a greater good. I suppose certain businesses benefit, at least in the short term, from a shady move by the leader. I believe leaders carry the responsibility of providing moral leadership. We can argue definitions of morality, but I do not believe that leaders should ever release themselves or others from their ethical responsibilities. I'm not sure how cunning and guile apply to those of us who lead in non-life-or-death situations, but I do know of the intrinsic value of standing for what is right.

PARADOXICAL LEADERSHIP

Paradox 4: Americans want powerful, self-confident presidential leadership; yet they are inherently suspicious of leaders who are arrogant and above criticism.

No matter what you thought about Ronald Reagan's politics, you have to agree that his navigation of this paradox was masterful. No president in my lifetime exuded more confidence in his political philosophy, nor has any president in my memory seemed more comfortable in laughing at his own pratfalls. This fusion of self-assurance and vulnerability may be why many people found Reagan's leadership impact greater than his success level.

Below, I discuss the importance of personal security as an indispensable element of 21st century leadership. I believe security serves as one of the important ties that bind confidence and humility. Although Cronin and Genovese present the American appetite for leaders with confidence but not arrogance as paradoxical, these two characteristics are commonly found in the truly secure leader. It is exactly the strong self-system that allows a leader to feel confident enough to get the job done, and secure enough to welcome criticisms that improve his or her performance.

Success in developing and displaying confidence without arrogance relies heavily, but not exclusively, on a healthy self-concept. Propelling leaders' movement between confidence and humility also requires a strong and honest self-awareness. There are some tasks in the life of our college that I do really well. They're jobs I've done many times and they play to my strengths. I'm the only one I want doing those jobs, and I think my co-workers share that opinion. In most jobs around the college, however, I would find myself two standard deviations below the mean in quality of performance, and I know my co-workers share that opinion. It is this self-awareness that enables my colleagues to believe that neither my confidence nor my humility is false or strategic. When former Boston Celtic star Larry Bird walked into the locker room before the first All-Star Game's three-point shooting contest, he called out, "Which one of you boys is gonna get second place this afternoon?" He then buried the competition. Larry Bird did not, however, pose that question or even enter the competition in the slam-dunk contest. The man had a love affair with gravity. Confidence and humility co-exist well together in leaders who know what they can and cannot do well

The federated authority of 21st century organizations places leader arrogance in direct conflict with the organizational structure and climate. Leaders neither can nor should "do it all." They must, however, have the ability and confidence to hold together the loosely bound units through which their missions are accomplished. Strength without arrogance enables them to meet the demands of the humble/confident leader paradox.

Paradox 5: Americans expect leaders to be visionary, but not unrealistic.

Most leaders get knocked for lacking vision or for being too idealistic. This paradox always seems to put a fat kid on the other side of our teeter-totter. Solomon had a point in observing, "Without a vision, the people perish."[6] We also accept Professor Noel Tichy's claim that "facing reality is the first crucial step that leaders must take."[7] Actually, these two poles aren't that far apart, which is why leaders don't have to drift very far from the middle before suffering the criticism of camping at one extreme or the other.

In my experience, the success of any attempt to unite vision and realism will rest on a fundamental premise—one that many failed leaders never understood. Leaders do not bring vision to an organization; rather, they extract a vision from it. Successful leaders dig into their organizations, mine the gold, and then figure out how and where to sell it. Having completed this painstaking exercise in reality, they trade in their picks and shovels for a chisel and begin to sculpt an image of what their enriched organizations can become. Bennis and Nanus are great on this point:

> In the end, the leader may be the one who articulates the vision and gives it legitimacy, who expresses the vision in captivating rhetoric that fires the imagination and emotions of followers....but if the organization is to be successful, the image must grow out of the needs of the entire organization and must be "claimed" or "owned" by all the important actors.[8]

Leaders must till their organizations for the makings of an achievable ideal. The people will recognize both the reality and the reach, and will feel ownership for both.

We need idealism from those we lead. I just returned from Amsterdam, where our family visited Corrie Ten Boom's hiding place where she protected Jews from their voracious Nazi predators. We were gloriously inspired by acts of heroism and strength. As I listened to the stories, I found myself thinking that the super-human acts of the stowaways were not really stories of the survival instinct; they were stories of hope. It was vision that kept the Jews from perishing in World War II. The manna of hope that they would one day embrace loved ones sustained them more than a primeval fear of loss of life and limb.

As leaders, we must provide visions that inspire hope. While visions may bound wildly about, true hope always settles within the latitudes of reality. Rare is the organization or group that exceeds the measurements of its leader's vision. But even more rare are the people who find hope in fanciful, unrealistic visions.

Three Ways to Traverse the Paradoxes

I feel very strongly that paradoxical leadership will serve 21st century organizations better than the unbending styles that provided comfort and predictability for yesterday's less-complicated enterprises. In offering the above paradoxes, I would like to suggest three rules for traversing them:

1. Go wide. Some who read this section on paradoxical leading will claim that I'm simply putting a new spin on the need for balance, which is hardly a new thought. They're wrong. Balance is achievable through timid baby steps, back and forth between two poles. I'm campaigning for a fat standard deviation—getting way out there in both directions. When it's time to be king don't be a wimp about it. Leave no doubt about who's running things. When it's time to be commoner lose the symbols of your office. The minute a leader gives the impression that being commoner for a few moments is an act of magnanimity, that leader is cooked. Leaders need to cut a wide berth in all the paradoxes of their roles, being "bipolar" in a healthy sense of the word.

2. Angle into the current. I've written most of this book lifting my eyes intermittently to watch the magnificent Pend Oreille River push north toward the fabled waters of the Columbia River. When I kayak on the Pend Oreille, I am never unaware that "going with the flow" will turn my kayak into a magneto. Any direction but north requires intention and effort. Paradoxical leaders must know the currents of their own preferences and personalities. Rarely will they find situational eddies that move them naturally upstream. For example, with respect to the "powerful but not too centralized" paradox, distributing authority comes more naturally to me than wielding it. Hence, I far more frequently ask myself the question, "Where do I need to engage?" than I ask, "Where am I micro-managing?" Centralizing power and exercising authority represent upstream actions for me. So occasionally I point my kayak in that direction, assuming that the currents of my style have carried me in the direction of decentralization. Leaders need to know where their comfort points lie on the paradoxical continuums of their positions, and they must be sure that they make moves toward the farthest pole. As a rule, angle upstream.

3. Don't become too predictable. In general, impact and predictability are inversely related. One of the great benefits of paradoxical leadership lies in the ability it provides the leader to avoid tight patterns. Leaders need to take advantage of the impact available to those who deploy bipolar acts. For the most part, distance from the opposite pole creates impact. Once at a dinner party, I finished eating before the other folks at our table, so I gathered everyone's dirty dishes and bussed the table. A couple of visitors considered my service salutary because of the distance it represented from my normal duties as president. Although my wife would break a dish over my head if I suggested dishes weren't in my job description, I guess for these folks, the surprise created impact. In another instance I saw some surprise-based impact at the opposite pole of this paradox when some students invited me (their buddy) to participate in an activity they'd dreamed up. Not only did I decline, I explained that they too would be declining. The message that I (now less their buddy) wanted them to hear managed to get around.

Leaders skilled in the paradoxes will recognize that the unexpected act packs more of a punch than the next stop in a standard pattern.

I suspect the ultimate paradox of leadership grows out of the longing people have for their leaders both to follow and lead them. Knowing when to reflect (follow) and when to shape (lead) the hopes and expectations of those we lead will determine the success with which we navigate the paradoxes. Some leaders will find it difficult to climb out of the troughs created by years of leading in a particular way. Others might reject paradoxical leadership as chaotic, if not duplicitous.

When I have succeeded in arcing polar opposites I have experienced a sense of wholeness. I am much more than someone's idea of a college president. In fact, only on the most formal of occasions am I comfortable in having anyone address me as anything other than "Bill." I do not wish to be narrowly known by my role (President Robinson) or my degree (Dr. Robinson). I love serious debate, and I love spontaneous laughter. I love to serve, and I love to be served. I love to teach, and I love to learn. In a sense, paradoxical leadership respects the glorious complexity of being made in the image of God. It is whole leadership for whole people.

Leading from the Middle

Paradoxical leadership does not work well from a distance. I often enter my office wearing cargo pants, an old sweatshirt and a baseball hat. None of my co-workers look twice. Once, when I was thus attired, I encountered an alum whom I had met only one time, and I had been wearing my starched-white-shirt-striped-tie-uniform. He was startled, apologizing that he had caught me on my day off. One of the women in the office quipped, "What are you talking about, he looks this way half the time." My clothes aren't very significant, but this incident makes the point. Leaders need to be close enough to their people so that when they appear at opposite poles of a paradox it isn't startling. It is in the middle of those they lead that leaders are granted the freedom that comes when their authenticity can be seen at close range. People know they go to the poles to be effective, not for effect.

REFLECTIONS:
Casting—Controlling Your Role

Soon after taking my place in my first president's chair, I began to fret about my image. On the first Saturday morning after classes began, I threw on some sweats, pulled a hat over my unwashed hair, hopped on my bike, and cruised over to the gym to check out our women's volleyball match. En route, I spotted an abandoned, half-consumed six-pack of beer (no doubt blown onto campus by strong winds) in a parking lot. I scooped it up and rode on. Predictably, a passerby in a car hollered, "Looking very presidential today aren't we?" Whatever it meant to look presidential, I was pretty sure I didn't.

I had decided that one of my most important tasks would be to shape a campus culture that would empower the accomplishment of our mission. What role should the president take in order to create a climate that would drive the mission? As a behavioral scientist, I had studied the force of roles. Their power continues to astonish me. In a sudden role shift, such as getting a phone call from our supervisor while we're conversing with a subordinate, we can almost physically feel our change in persona. In my first year as a college president, I learned that whoever took charge of casting my role would shape the environment. I needed to understand my role repertoire and cast myself in the roles that were appropriate for the moment and the mission. There were many "directors" on campus. Sometimes unwittingly, sometimes intentionally, they cast me into roles that would serve their purposes. I discovered that my institutional perspective and self-awareness put me in the best position to choose the appropriate role. Sometimes the role I chose coincided with the ways in which others were trying to cast me; sometimes it did not. The battle was in my taking control of my self-perception.

Two discoveries followed. First, I realized that there are many roles that can be used to do a job effectively; hence, I probably worried too much about finding a "correct" role. As it turns out, my general approach to overseeing a college developed into one quite different from those of any of my friends who do this job. Second, my experience confirmed the theory that there is a predictable synchrony resulting from the roles we choose. Others see us in the way we see ourselves; others feel comfortable with us when we are comfortable with ourselves; others feel confident in us when we feel confident in ourselves. Our social environment takes on mirror qualities. How we see ourselves has a profound impact on how others see us. We need a mindset in which we think of our position in terms of holding the reins on roles that lead to effectiveness.

Chapter 3
Secure Leadership

O f the six qualities, security and virtue probably transcend eras more than the other four. Current trends push their value higher than ever. For example, leading today's decentralized organizations by remote control is not a job for the paranoid leader. This situation will result in a race to see who goes crazy first, the leader or the led.

Through the ages, group members have enjoyed being led by secure people. I define a secure leader as "the person motivated to meet the task and needs of the group rather than personal needs." I once met with a trustee to seek advice about an administrator whose leadership was proving very ineffective. At one point, the trustee looked at me and said, "You're offended by his insecurity, aren't you?"

The question caught me off guard. Offended? I responded with, "I guess I am," but I had to take that question home and think about it. She was right. I was offended that this person put meeting his needs in front of meeting the needs of those whom he he'd been charged to lead. The first time he co-opted credit for a faculty member's accomplishments, the group cut him some slack. The second time, they skinned him. Both times it made me mad. If we were to examine the causes of leadership failure by adding up all the bad luck, bad group members, and leader incompetence, the sum of the causes wouldn't come close to the number of leaders felled by their own ego needs.

Insecurity surfaces at the extremes. Generally, bravado, timidity, and micro-management serve as the most visible portals of insecurity. They do not work for the leader, especially in the new culture. Increasingly decentralized structures require leaders to be confident and spacious. Centricity must be distributed enthusiastically, rather than cautiously guarded by the timid or lodged in the ego of the proud. Caution and egocentricity keep the center too close to the leader in today's business environment. I offer two suggestions for the leader trying to become more secure:

Let Go to Go

One simple perception, more than any other, will determine the longevity and effectiveness of a leader. Secure leaders recognize:

> Leading is not about me. Letting go of my recognition, my image, my control, and my self-interest will free me to grasp my responsibility. My duty is to see that this organization executes its mission with excellence and strength. Any needs I have to be the star or marionette of that execution steal from this organization and misdirect my energy. When I let go of me, my role changes. I become the dispatcher rather than the driver, the coach rather than the player, the resource rather than the watchdog, and the interpreter rather than the expert. If I stick to my self-concept of strategist, spokesperson, and inspirer, I can survive this job for a few more years. But if everything's all about me, I will buckle under the weight of my own frailties and needs. It's too hard to keep my ego fed. The more it gets, the more it wants.

Our habits and our reflexes fake us into hanging on to credit when we should let go. The folks in most fund-raising operations get suckered both by habits and reflexes. They may be wonderful, talented people, but they work in an industry that uses "credit-grasping" language. Virtually all fund-raisers use it, myself included. For example, in reporting on a capital campaign, fund-raisers will tell a group of donors "We've raised $88 million toward our goal." Do those donors want to hear how good we are, or how good they are? Why wouldn't fund-development people say "To date, friends of the college have given $88 million?"

Credit-taking language is a bad habit, formed by talking mostly to each other. But reflexes also pitch in. When fundraisers report the fruits of their hard work, it really does feel like they raised the money and that they should get kudos for their efforts. They work hard to help make people generous. So they give themselves a few pats on the back. This very act defeats its own purpose. When I hear a self-congratulatory tone from someone, I don't need to say, "Good job"—they already took care of that.

Empowering others is another area of letting go that secure leaders handle more easily than their insecure counterparts. I suspect that secure leaders delegate responsibility where insecure leaders delegate jobs. In my own situation, I have never really discussed with my direct reports their perceptions of their responsibilities. I can't believe I haven't done this. Do the people reporting to me feel their duties have been given to them by me or by their job descriptions and the mission of the organization? Am I secure enough to say it's the latter; that they work for the organization and not for me? Or is our relationship such that they push beyond their job descriptions to help me? I need to schedule a few conversations about empowerment.

The 21st century CEO must serve as the agent for the overall organization by empowering and equipping unit leaders to charge forward. Insecure leaders who delegate jobs while keeping a tight rein on their people will look like maypoles. Tethered people will adoringly run in circles around them, while the competition gleefully runs circles around their organizations.

Don't Believe Andre

I've read numerous accounts of tennis great Andre Agassi's professional turning point coming when he stopped believing his own line that "Image is everything." If Agassi stopped believing Agassi, so should the rest of us. William James defined *self-esteem* as the "numerator of success over the denominator of pretension." I'm not sure these two variables are best represented as a fraction, but I am sure that lowering pretense raises the odds of successful leadership.

I work in an industry that specializes in pretense. We present ourselves to society as liberal champions of the powerless. We demand justice and egalitarianism. But just let those powerless proletarians try addressing us without our lofty titles and we'll drop a load of condescension on them like they've never seen before. We rank our faculty members and call ourselves doctors. Mind you, it's not pretense. We are a humble folk, seeking only to preserve respect for the positions we occupy, not for ourselves. Yikes. We're not only full of ourselves, we're dishonest about it. Actually, academia is improving, but it fell for a logic that has never made sense to me. I am baffled by this business of respecting positions more than people. Bill Clinton commits immoral acts that would turn 99 percent of the supervisors in America into erstwhile supervisors in less than a second, but we deferred to Clinton because of his office. Meanwhile, we treat hard-working, moral people as if they were disposable because they work in "low-life" jobs. I find this practice short on logic and long on pretense.

Leaders must feel secure enough to quit worshipping the Baal of image. People need real leaders, not Madison Avenue creations or self-saturated potentates. What we wear, how we're dressed, the size of our offices, and how we're addressed all serve to expand or reduce the distance between ourselves and those we lead.

We need to see our people and ourselves in functional rather than hierarchical roles. This perceptual shift flows in the direction of organizational movement today. Moreover, it can reinforce our efforts to empower people. I have a relatively large office compared to other people where I work. One day while visiting another college president in his palatial office, I thought "What a waste to burn all this space on presidents who are gone half the time." (Like many people, I'm much better at seeing others' faults than my own.) A couple months later, we bought the kind of workstation in which I could hide my computer, phone, and junk piles, and then we converted the rest of my office into a conference room. Now, people schedule this conference room for meetings whenever I am out of town. I'm sure nobody is thinking, "Well, he's not the leader we thought he was if he's willing to let people use his office."

A number of years ago, I pulled together the search committee for a very important position. I asked what they would choose as the most important quality we should seek. The first response was, "someone who is comfortable with him or herself." Leaders making waves in the new century will put mission and people well ahead of meeting their own personal needs. It shouldn't be that hard, but it makes a big difference.

Leading from the Middle

My grandfather instilled in me a love for the cello, and Anne Martindale Williams, principal cellist of the Pittsburgh Symphony for the past 25 years, is my favorite cellist in all the world. I love Yo-Yo Ma and Rostrpovich, but I'd rather hear Anne. First, I hear God in her bow. Second, during my doctoral studies of organizational leadership, Anne taught me about the "middle." At that time, she, her husband Joe, and my wife Bonnie would do chamber music programs, so we became very good friends. During Advent of 1979, I invited a bunch of my crazy, tone-deaf friends to come over to the house for a Christmas carol party. For this crew, the operative word in the invitation was "party." I had somehow conned Bonnie into accompanying our "chorus" and almost facetiously invited Anne and Joe to come over. "Sure," Anne replied, "should we bring our instruments?"

This woman, who spent her Friday nights four feet to the right of conductor Andre Previn, who paid three times more for her cello than for their house, was offering to cast her pearls before my musically sub-swine friends. As I sat in our tiny living room watching her roar with laughter and play with a virtuosity that not ten other living cellists could match, I realized that she was every bit as comfortable in the middle of regular people as in the front of the Pittsburgh Symphony. Such security just magnified the power of her selflessness. When Anne was in the middle, she cared nothing of image, nothing of impressing others, nothing of anything other than giving a gift to her friends.

Today's leaders must be secure enough to be seen and known up close. They must put themselves so close to those they lead that pretense becomes impossible. When they walk into the middle, they communicate a confidence that respect is not about image and posturing. Silently they announce that they are not afraid to be known.

REFLECTIONS:
LETTING GO

Somehow this past year I said good-bye to a couple things that needed to go. Of course, I would look like Lot's pillarized wife if a granule of salt were added for every time I've looked back. Maybe letting go of looking back can be my next project.

I'm convinced that we can't "go" if we don't "let go." Last week I found myself playing in a big three-on-three basketball tournament with my 18-year-old son, Ben, and his two 18-year-old friends. We were in the "18 to 24-year old, 6'2" and under" division. The tournament, Spokane's Hoopfest, has a provision that allows you to play on a team if you're so much older than 24 that you can't possibly help the team. I was a shoe-in on that basis, not to mention the fact that in the last year my entire body has totally crashed. I've played in this tournament, in the appropriate age category, with friends for the last five years. But this year I was not with my peers, and in a flash of uncharacteristic maturity, I knew I would have to leave behind my self-assigned star status. I had a new role, the only role that made sense, but a role that was foreign to me—tag-along. It worked. The fifth wheel was the one Ben needed me to be. It was the "dad wheel." For me to excel as father, I had to let go of my self-image in basketball.

Being a parent of my dear daughters, Brenna and Bailley, forces me to deal with "letting go." When Brenna headed off to college, it made my eyes squirt, but I didn't have to let go of my fundamental relationship with her. However, I fear that when either of these women presents me with some guy who will replace me as the Number One man in her life, it's my heart that will do the squirting. That will be serious letting go.

Giving up elements of our personal and professional life will free us for personal and professional growth. Professionally, I had to let go of one image and two attitudes this year. I had an image of our college that was destroying my objectivity. It was my picture, and I was the president, both of the picture and the college. In our institutional-planning process, I kept looking at our needs and opportunities on the canvas of my vision. I realized that for me to know if my picture was the best one for the future of this college, I had to let it go. With me as its easel not too many shots were going to be fired at it. So I backed off, and the result is that my colleagues and I are going into the new year excited about painting a great picture, which may or may not look like the one I was hauling around. We may reach a point where I have to say, "This is how it's going to be," but it won't be before we start. My next challenge will be to keep from checking the rear-view mirror if we move to new ideas that resemble little of the vision I let go.

Providing good leadership also requires us to lose a few attitudes. The ones that needed to go for me were related to a couple of my co-workers. Their values were so different from mine that it was hard for me to feel good about their work, even though they were meeting my productivity expectations. I was cautious in affirming their successes, getting caught up in their styles rather than seeing their results. So, I let go of the "Be like me" attitude . . .sort of. And it's better . . . sort of. Hopefully, I can lose "sort of."

Chapter 4
Inspiring Leadership

W*hen Aeschines spoke, the people remarked, "How well he speaks." But when Demosthenes spoke, the people cried out, "Let us march against Phillip!"*

I have no idea who uttered this line, but it is my favorite quote from five years of doctoral study. I'm a sucker for inspiration. I don't care if leadership scholars feed inspiration to the dinosaurs, the chances of me following will skyrocket when the leader inspires me.

To inspire is to propel people to action. It is to deliver a compelling vision of what could be. Inspiring relies less on authoring the vision than on being able to deliver it straight to the soul. Granted, being the visionary may add to the impact, but people can inspire on many bases other than "I thought this up." I have an African-American friend who misspeaks occasionally when offering spontaneous remarks. But when he launches into Martin Luther King, Jr.'s "I Have a Dream" speech, you understand what it means to listen with your blood. The last time I heard him give it—through my tears, goose bumps, and shame—I silently vowed to march relentlessly against the "Phillip" of racism.

The Greek translation of *inspire* is "to breathe into." The inspirational leader breathes energy and life into the people being led. Leaders in the 21st century will most often deliver inspiration in the form of passionately communicating how to fill the gap between what is and what could be. Both organizations and individuals must understand how to bridge the distance between the status quo and their full potential. It is not enough for leaders to point the way;

they must stir the passions of those they lead. I have never seen a corporate leader do a better job of putting fire in the belly of his people than Don Barbieri, CEO of Spokane-based WestCoast Hospitality Corporation. He paints the ideal, then through consistency, relentlessness and his own passion, he convinces all who will listen that the ideal is not idealistic—it is achievable.

I love the way James Kouzes and Barry Posner use the Greek translation of "inspire" to define this essential dimension of a leader's responsibility.

> Leaders breathe life into the hopes and dreams of others and enable them to see the exciting possibilities that the future holds. Leaders forge a unity of purpose by showing constituents how the dream is for the common good. Leaders can't ignite the flame of passion in others if they don't express enthusiasm for the compelling vision of their group.[1]

While sitting here thinking about inspiration, I just heard a Scottish piper blow strains of an old hymn that carried me back 10 years to a dying young woman. In an astonishing act of leadership, she breathed life into those of us allowed to enter the sanctuary of her final days. Shortly after the oncologist handed Suzanne a four-to-six-weeks sentence, she built a furious to-do list, with "The Party," exactly six weeks out, at the top of her list. Suzanne had no intention of "going gentle into that good night." She would be at that party, and there was a ton to be done. So Suzanne built a program through which she would indefatigably lead us as she left us. The scene of the culminating party was a beach house in Laguna Beach, California, where she spent her final weeks a stone's throw from the cove where *Beaches* was filmed.

On the day of the party, Bonnie and I arrived at John Wayne Airport in the early afternoon, and were scheduled to depart at 6 a.m. the following morning. The event was grand. Suzanne took control, not so much of us, but of the atmosphere from which she deftly removed both denial and misery. By 2 a.m., exhaustion had conquered all but Suzanne, Bonnie and me. For the next three hours, this brilliant 23-year-old Princeton graduate conducted a clinic on life. As the time drew near for our final embrace with Suzanne, I asked her, "What have you learned in the last six weeks?" With the quiet confidence of a woman who had seen more of life's mysteries than most people thrice her age, she replied, "That what we learn isn't as important as what we *do* with what we learn." The night before her funeral, which she had asked me to conduct, I woke up at 3 a.m. and sobbed helplessly, as I had five months earlier when we'd learned the cancer she had once beaten was back. But I did not cry when we said our final goodbye. I remember, almost with guilt, that as I held Suzanne before leaving for the airport, I felt a greater sense of duty than grief. Suzanne knew we would never see each other again, but she did not give me a teary-eyed goodbye, she commissioned me to "do with what I've learned."

God forbid that I write anything here that trivializes the memory of this precious woman. Suzanne breathed life into me. She moved us to action. She called us to be doers. Like all good leaders, Suzanne took risks, made mistakes, and failed in a few efforts as her end drew near, due partially to her lifeline of steroids. But she donned the mantle of leadership in a way that dwarfed her frailties and flaws. Suzanne, ever a leader, seized the moment to inspire, and she taught us what the word means.

Today's leaders compete with complacency, distraction and a bombardment of fingertip diversions that tug on their people. Loyalty, honor and duty can atrophy beneath the fast-paced tedium of simply keeping up with life. But when we breathe energy into these dormant virtues, people will rise to the specifications of our vision. They will "march against Phillip."

Leading from the Middle

People who lead from the middle are able to inspire not only with their messages, but also through their lives. I worked for a provost named Glenn Heck, a brilliant man whose throwaway comments were better than most people's best orations. Almost everything he said inspired me. Glenn made no effort to distance himself from those of us who reported to him. We knew him well, and he knew us well. Quite by coincidence, but because we were so close to Glenn, I learned about an incredibly sacrificial gift that he and his wife had very quietly made to their church. The discovery utterly inspired me. It added moral authority to everything Glenn had spoken. For most of us, our ability to inspire rests more in the way we go about our work and live our lives than in our rhetorical skills.

One morning we found a note left by a student that I invited to stay in our home during finals week. His living situation made it hard for him to study, so we offered him the spare bedroom. I don't know if any of my convocation addresses over the past three years of his college career have in any way inspired this guy, but according to his note, living with us for a week did. St. Francis is said to have urged his followers, "At all times preach the gospel, and when necessary, use words."

Inspiring Leadership

REFLECTIONS:
MY BAD

I play basketball several times each week. It's good exercise and it reminds me of something I used to do well. In basketball, there's a floor language to which all players are privy and that no non-playing spectator could imagine. One of the most frequent utterances on the court follows an error in judgment when the guilty party moans, "My bad." This admission is especially forthcoming when there could be some argument over whose "bad" it really was. For example, a stolen pass can be thrown too softly or to the wrong side of the receiver. However, if the receiver doesn't move toward the ball as it is thrown, it gives the defender the split second needed for a steal.

"My bad" immediately prompts the confessor into a) working harder to make up for his or her "bad," b) concentrating on not making the same "bad" again, and c) showing the team that he or she takes responsibility for a mistake. All of these things are good.

I think people in leadership have to form a "my bad" mental reflex that kicks in whenever there's a problem. Whether we're thinking in terms of our organization or ourselves, we must ask what we could have done better. Last month I sat with two angry parents who felt their child had been ill treated in one of our co-curricular activities. At one point I mused, "It doesn't sound to me like we handled that particular situation very well." I was almost thinking out loud to myself. What followed is interesting:

1) The parents softened, and we had a more objective discussion.

2) I later made it a point to speak with the overseer of that co-curricular area to see if, indeed, we hadn't handled the situation very well.

3) I discovered that we had dealt with the student in a reasonably sensitive and supportive way, but the supervisor and I did find a couple areas in which we fell short of the ideal.

4) The supervisor decided to discuss in general this shortcoming in their department retreat.

5) I saw the student in question, and I worked hard to make up for what might have been a weakness in our handling of his situation.

One "my bad" produced at least five "goods."

Chapter 5

Communicative Leadership

Recently, I was having lunch with two college presidents. We were whining about this and that when one of them quipped, "When I retire I'm going to consult for college presidents. And before I set foot on any campus, I will have already written, 'After careful analysis I have concluded that you need to communicate more with the board and with your employees.' Trustees and faculty will hail my insight, and everyone will be dazzled by my speed." He can't miss.

For a while I thought the information age might sate our appetite for communication. I thought wrong. Technology is creating exponential advances in communication. I have two graduate degrees in communication, but I'm still not sure that I understand the revolution that is taking place. Effective communication may be the most basic requirement of the 21st century leader. Today's leader who says, "I tried everything to reach you but we couldn't seem to connect" will be sporting a seriously long nose. With current tools, anyone can communicate, and efforts will leave a trail. The only reason for not communicating with those whom we lead is our choice not to.

One of the most important steps leaders can take in becoming better communicators begins with the recognition that the phrase, "What we have here is a failure to communicate," made famous in the movie *Cool Hand Luke*, is always wrong. What leaders have is not a failure to communicate, but a failure to communicate effectively.

I try to operate on the assumption that we never fail to communicate; we just fail to communicate the messages we intend to. We need to view the receivers of our messages as sovereign. Ultimately, their filters and their perceptions present them with advice on which of our messages they will receive. Our job is to wrap our messages in clarity. Effective communication is a match between the message intended and the message heard.

I used to write subtle and respectful, non-pushy gift appeals. Actually, I still do, but four years into my life as a college president I got smacked with the awareness that my letters were communicating the wrong message to some people. A man said to me, "I don't even open my mail from you anymore. The only time I ever hear from you is when you want my money." So in February 1990 I started writing monthly newsletters to alumni, friends, and parents, of our students. I throw all kinds of news into these Kiplinger-type letters, but I never say too much about our financial needs. I've received far more thanks for these 2,500-word notes than for anything else I've done in my professional life. The information represents just one of the messages that people receive when they get the newsletter. I've learned that when I get done writing one of these informal, and occasionally irreverent, letters I'd better edit it for between-the-lines messages. I've been scolded both for what I did say, for what I didn't say, and for what that communicated. I've learned a great deal about communication from this monthly discipline.

The 21st century leader faces formidable communication interference and competition. Skill and persistence in communicating effectively will correlate directly with a leader's success. Leaders will have to think not only about message-sending, but they will also need to study the communication environments in which messages are flying back and forth. The message constitutes only one part of the communication process. Something in an e-mail I once sent cast a co-worker into a tailspin that came perilously close to a crash. The only sin of the message was ambiguity that I could have easily clarified. But because: 1) we weren't communicating regularly, 2) I thought we'd communicated successfully and I did not pick up on a problem, 3) we were really busy, and 4) my co-worker chose to deal with my misguided communication without questioning me, my colleague anguished for several months. This is a case in which the communication environment contributed more to our difficulties than the actual message culprit did.

The above mess of misunderstanding demonstrates how listening holds equal status to sending messages in the communication process. Unfortunately, our culture tends to value effective speaking more than it values good listening. Leaders looking to make durable contributions to their groups will always be listening and looking for significant messages. Sometimes we hear about the leader who is a "good communicator, but doesn't listen well." There is no such animal. The good leader who doesn't listen resembles the good driver who frequently ends up at the wrong place. Leaders who communicate well listen, probe, read, study and respect their various audiences. Communication is not simply the act of sending messages.

The Top Six Listening Conclusions

The best way for us to learn is to ask questions, but we need to listen to more than just the answers to our questions. We need to be in a listening frame of mind. I have a pastor friend who does something amazing. When you speak to him, he closes his mouth, looks you in the eye, nods as you're talking, asks you a question or two to make sure he understands, and, as near as I can tell, cares about what you say to him. I find this behavior startling but impressive. He's definitely a collector's item—someone who listens and learns.

Because I want to be more like my friend, I've thought a lot about listening. Here are my top six conclusions about listening:

1. People like to be heard. There is a gap between what I have learned about listening and how well I do it. When it comes to listening, people give you more points for doing than for understanding.

2. We should listen twice as much as we speak. There's a reason God gave us two ears and one mouth. Do the math.

3. We are conditioned socially to not listen. In an age of extraordinary information overload, tuning out has become a basic means of survival. Interference has become so relentless that it is very difficult to discriminate between the message and all the noise.

4. *Listening is more of an attitude than a skill.* I discovered this principle when I was in prison—visiting. I was giving a seminar in 1980 at the Anamosa State Penitentiary in rural Iowa. It was a level-IV prison primarily for violent offenders. As I was about to walk into a room, I glanced down at the sign-in sheet. What I saw stopped me in my tracks. More than 75 six-digit numbers, no sign of a name. As I walked to the front of the room and looked at rows of desperate faces, I decided if I didn't do anything else that weekend, I would learn and use every prisoner's name. I couldn't wait to hear each man announce the name that had been taken away from him, and to my amazement, those names stuck like glue in my mind. In reflecting on this experience, I realized that when I really care, I really listen.

5. *The best measures of the attitude behind your listening are the frequency and depth of your inquisitiveness.* If, in our efforts to become better listeners, we do not start with our attitudes toward whomever or whatever we need to hear, we will simply become better imposters. We would be more honest to simply say, "Good afternoon, I have become quite skilled at faking interest in what you have to say." Or, "Good afternoon, I'm about to listen only to your ideas that will reinforce what I have already decided." Or, "Good afternoon, I am about to pay the price of listening to you briefly in order that I might inform you, not so briefly." Ambrose Bierce, in *The Devil's Dictionary*, defines heaven as "a place where the wicked cease from troubling you with talk of their personal affairs, and the good listen with attention while you expound your own." Do you question, do you probe, do you dig, do you care?

6. *Listening requires preparation.* We should be as thoughtful about preparing to listen as we are about preparing a speech. Good listening requires preparation, concentration, and reflection. Get ready to hear, focus on your source, and then review what you heard.

The Listener's Toolbox

Listed below are my communication axioms for 21st century leaders. Whoever follows these rules will provide leadership, whether in a position of authority or not.

Casting pearls is not a smart way for leaders to treat communication. Communication is a transaction, not an action. Leaders need to consider the simultaneous interaction of themselves, their messages, the channels they use, and their intended receivers when they communicate.

Communicating too often is a better mistake than not communicating often enough. Initiating the communication process invites feedback while providing group members with awareness and understanding. Most leaders do not communicate with group members as often as they feel they do.

You are a poor judge of your listening skills. Most leaders try to lead conversations, and often they're the only ones in the room who aren't listening. You can't lead a conversation well without spending most of your time listening.

It's better to be insultingly clear than respectfully unclear. Don't be afraid of spelling things out. One of the biggest communication obstacles for leaders is that they know what they mean; hence, their ability to judge their clarity is compromised.

Words are overrated. We expect too much from words. A word is simply an abstract symbol until a human being attaches some meaning. We get into trouble when we think words possess universal meaning, (what "no" means to me is not what "no" means to my 18-year-old). Assume words are clues to what we mean—give as many clues as necessary.

Questions are underrated. Leaders need to be listeners, and the best listeners are always skilled questioners. They've come to terms with the shortcomings of words and with the way their own filters can tweak a message. They don't assume that they have grasped your meaning, so they probe and clarify. These are the people we love to be around, because they seem to care about understanding our favorite topic—ourselves.

Inferences are risky. When my brother was a sophomore in high school, he went through the terrifying experience of being served liver while dining at a friend's house. In an enormous act of courage, he fought off gag reflexes and choked down the slimy organ in a couple of painful swallows. Dear Mrs. Carmean, mistaking politeness for enjoyment, insisted he have the last piece. His protests were futile; she could just tell that he really liked liver. Asking and believing always serve us better than assuming we understand.

Effective communication is powerful. Somehow, imperfect messengers using imprecise terms manage to communicate through our perceptual fortresses with the power to absolutely inspire or devastate us. When we do communicate effectively, the results justify almost any amount of effort required.

Empathizing improves responding. One of the primary ways that I've defined my own maturity is by periodically measuring the amount of time it takes a thought entering my head to come barging out of my mouth. Thinking about how the person with whom we're communicating will hear our next expression can transform our message-sending effectiveness.

Thinking the best is the best kind of thinking. There's a lot of guesswork involved in communication. When we don't have all the information we need about other people, we just guess. When we think the best with our guesses, we convey trust and optimism. When we make uncharitable assumptions about others, we convey mistrust and cynicism. Which leader would you want to follow?

Giving Feedback

C.K. Chesterton once said, "If something's worth doing, it's worth doing badly." I think he was referring to various confessions of the soul. If you need to say you're sorry, it's better to stumble through a poorly expressed apology than remain silent because you don't know what to say. Chesterton's aphorism applies to many communication opportunities. As it relates to feedback, even ineptly expressed performance feedback, if respectful, is better than no feedback at all. We simply can't make smart adjustments in our efforts if we don't have feedback mechanisms. Organizations with a "cybernetic culture"(one in which feedback helps us chart our course as we go) stay nimble and adaptive.

I served as youth pastor in a magnificent Presbyterian church in downtown Pittsburgh during my doctoral studies. One Sunday, after I'd been greeting folks as they scrambled out of the sanctuary (churches welcome people to enter, then make them stand in line to leave), the senior pastor told me I wasn't focused during my per-

70

functory, "God bless you, don't let the door hit you on the way out" routine. In fact, he claimed I was looking down the line to see if anyone interesting had picked my less-crowded door. I learned later that my brother-in-law had been his informant. I could not have known at the time that no small part of my living would be made pumping hands, but to this day, every time my duties call on me to greet folks individually, I hear echoes of that very helpful feedback.

Chesterton was right. Feedback is so important that any direct, well-intentioned expression probably helps. But direct feedback is not an easy skill to develop. There are, however, a few basic feedback instincts that we can adopt:

Mixing the peas with the mashed potatoes. I've found that holding corrective feedback until I have affirming feedback can take the bad taste out of sessions in which I'm asking for changes. Timing is everything. Held too long, negative feedback is difficult for the hearer to put into context, and it loses the impact of immediacy. Instant correction, however, feels like nagging. If we try to soften the instantaneous correction with some kind of gold star that we quickly think up, we can send a mixed message that is difficult for others to sort out while they're in the throes of what it is we're correcting. I find that regularly scheduled meetings are the ideal time to provide accumulated feedback, both affirming and corrective.

Assuming good intentions. As a young academic dean, I had to tell a faculty member that her co-workers found her very defensive. In trying to think of some nice way to rebuild her self-system, which I was about to dismantle, I stumbled upon her heart. This woman was the most loyal faculty member in our division, and she fired both barrels on anyone who criticized us or her efforts to make us better. So I sat down with this woman in a different frame of mind than as if I were about the task of explaining how distasteful people found her defective character. I assumed that she wanted to grow, which in fact she did. She acknowledged that considering questions and criticisms as threats, rather than as ways to improve, had impeded her development.

Channeling my sensitivity. The one thing I hate worse than getting my feelings hurt is hurting someone else's feelings. I'm distressingly sensitive to criticism, so I'm reluctant to say things to others that could be hurtful. I've found I can use this sensitivity in a positive way if I apply it to how, not whether, I give feedback. Discipline is required for me to take the feedback step, but I can take the step confidently if I know I'll be sensitive in delivering the message. Rather than allowing such situations to make me cower, I try to use my sensitivity to give me boldness. I'm sure there are those who err on the bold side, but for the most part, leaders and managers give too little, not too much, feedback.

We need to think of feedback as a map. Our employees and our organizations must know when they're headed in the right direction and when they deviate—and so must we. The leaders who hold a deep value for feedback will create cybernetic climates that can keep our organizations on course.

Leading from the Middle

In the 21st century, I do not expect we will often hear the description of someone as a "strong leader but weak communicator." To be sure, we will encounter leaders with limited skills in public speaking or writing or even in interpersonal communication. But all effective leaders will have at least one communication tool in their kits with which they can proclaim their dreams and visions with penetrating power. Messages communicated weakly will never be heard amid the sheer volume of information rushing through the ever-expanding channels of communication.

We find ourselves in a new age. Information and learning have taken over cultures once dominated by mining and manufacturing. The power of leaders has been distributed throughout more federated groups and organizations. People weave cocoons to protect themselves from information bombardments. Everything about contemporary society raises the stakes for leaders to communicate effectively. I wonder how many of the people I lead find themselves in turbulent situations and desperately need me to communicate with them. Some people characterize me as a good communicator, but no matter how skilled I might be, I'm not a good communicator if my silence sends out messages of negligence. If we wish to lead people, we must manage messages and manage them well.

Communicative Leadership

Almost all of today's communication textbooks present the evolution of communication theory as moving from an action model (message sent one direction), to an interaction model (messages sent back and forth), and then to a transaction model (message exchanged simultaneously). To me, these three models represent rungs of communication quality. Several days ago I sent a message by e-mail to our students (action model). I received a note back from a student named Amber, saying she would like to meet with me; so I sent her a note back (interaction model) urging her to stop me the next time she saw me. The next day Amber approached me in the Union Building and introduced herself. Our short conversation was very pleasant for both of us (transactional model). The potential for transactional communication rises sharply when leaders are visible and accessible. Not only does being in the middle increase the frequency of direct communication transactions, it puts us in a better position to manage the meaning of our messages when we are forced to use the action approach. Today, only "Wizard of Oz" leaders can stay behind the curtain—and as we know, that doesn't work forever.

REFLECTIONS:
SENDING A MESSAGE

Years ago, my brother sent his five-year-old son next door to see if the neighbors had an extra half-cup of sugar. An hour later his son wandered back home and announced, "Yup, they have extra sugar." So brother Ed asks, "Where were you and where's the sugar?" His son shrugged and muttered, "You didn't say you wanted it."

We can influence, but not control, how we communicate. Ultimately, our audience decides what we have communicated. For that reason, I try to err on the side of saying too much rather than too little (which is no news flash to my co-workers). The method, time, attitude, and substance of what we communicate all send messages. Recognizing that the receiver of these messages probably has scramblers inside both ears makes it important for us to work toward making sure that what is heard matches what we want to say. We need to think about what our audience will do with a message. Many times our primary message doesn't appear in the substance of the communication. We rely on subtext to be our courier. Just like in the example of my brother, we allow our audience the power of inferring what they will with our message. People in positions of leadership need to think about the messages they're sending—and the ones they're not sending. I try to have a plan, a philosophy and a policy that guide me.

The danger of inference is that we take into account what we assume to be our audience's intentions. This can result in the immediate defensive posturing of those who listen to us. A couple of months ago, I served on a committee that was dealing with a personnel issue. Over the course of our deliberations we received a letter in which the writer criticized our process in a way that was factual and fair, reflecting his different opinion of the best method for approaching this decision. The letter concluded, however, by saying something to the effect of, "Obviously, you had made up your minds going into this." This conclusion riled the committee because he entered the sanctuary of our motives. Had this critic said, "It feels to me as if you had made up your minds before you started," I'm certain the criticism would have stung, but we would have received it differently. There's something sacred about people's motives. We should allow them the opportunity to identify what those motives are. The only other pathway available is through inference, and it doesn't always lead to the right place.

If we can overcome our own tendencies to infer the unspoken message, then we will be able to express ourselves much more effectively. A formula that has helped me control my inferences can be thought of as a "tentativeness index." Typically, we make an observation, then draw an inference, and finally form a judgment. For example, "I haven't seen Al at work this week" (observation). "He must be on vacation" (inference). "This is a bad time for Al to be taking off" (judgment). In my tentativeness index, the closer you get to judgment, the more tentative you need to become. The fact that you haven't seen Al at work is a simple observation that requires little tentativeness, unless your short-term memory range is less than a week. But when you put Al on vacation, you're moving into inferential whitewater. He could be at a conference or working in a different office, or there might be any number of other options. So this inference must be held tentatively. Finally, when you're two steps away from your observation and you are judging Al for his choice of vacation time, you need to be so tentative that it's hardly worth worrying about.

Drawing inferences requires skill and should not be thought of negatively; in fact, it is more efficient than requiring complete information on everything we observe. But it is supremely dangerous, not to mention arrogant, to assume that our powers to infer are so great that they rank right up there with the facts. We need to operate in a frame of mind that differentiates an inference from a fact, and then proceed with the appropriate level of tentativeness.

Chapter 6
Virtuous Leadership

In December 1991, through a series of bizarre circumstances, I tracked down NBA basketball player and Indiana basketball legend Steve Alford and hired him as coach for Manchester College's 0-6 men's basketball team. Starting his fifth year in the NBA, Steve had just been cut from a West Coast team and was in conversation with the Boston Celtics. I'd read that he ultimately wanted to be a college coach and did not like the NBA lifestyle very much. We had a sudden vacancy, so with a "what have I got to lose" attitude, I called Steve. Within 36 hours of my first contact we shook hands, and three days later the most beloved basketball figure in the America's most basketball-crazed state had moved with his great (and pregnant) wife, Tanya, to North Manchester, Indiana.

After watching Steve for one week of practice, I concluded that he would become a very good college coach. After watching him for a month, I thought he might also become a very good leader. Then on Monday, May 18, 1992, I thought, "This guy might become a great leader."

It was the morning after the Alfords got home from the hospital with their newborn child, and I dashed over to their house to meet baby Kory. Everything was typical new parents/new baby stuff until the new dad and I walked out to my car. In a light rain, Steve said, "I want to thank you."

Although his words were a bit halting, I thought he was thanking me for stopping by. "Are you kidding?" I replied, "I wanted to see Kory."

Then he said, "I'm not talking about that. I want to thank you that I'm here. If I had signed with the Celtics, I might have been in Cleveland (where the Celtics were playing the Cavaliers in the NBA playoffs) and missed seeing my son being born. Can you imagine how horrible that would have been?"

What I could scarcely imagine was that this 27-year-old, who dreamed every day of his Hoosier childhood of playing in the NBA, felt that seeing the birth of his son was much more important than being a professional basketball player. It was then that I knew he really meant what he said about his values.

When a leader's virtue rebuffs culture's most seductive invitations, the power of authenticity is created—and it is a power that can catapult or destroy leadership. Maybe I shouldn't have been so taken, but if one of *Grimm's Fairy Tale* fairies had asked me, at age 27, to choose between playing in an NBA playoff or seeing my child arrive in the world, I don't even want to know what I would have said. Virtue in leadership gives people the confidence that nothing expedient or self-gratifying can ever divert their leader from doing what is right and good.

If my list of 21st century leadership qualities falls victim to wishful thinking at any point, it is here. In a couple of years, I will hit the number-two spot in longevity of the Whitworth College presidents. This endurance should get me at least a couple of pages in the next written history of the college. (This recognition inspires me to work hard at kissing up to the college historian.) No doubt my two pages will refer to buildings, money, enrollment, and how weird it was to have a president whose maturity level was indistinguishable from that of the students. But what I want most in those two pages is for someone to remember me as a really good person. My target is to be the kind of leader my children imagine me to be. I want to be a leader known for my virtues as well as for my accomplishments.

I hold a somewhat confused perspective on virtue and ethics, but I hold it tenaciously. I'm even more dogmatic about virtue now than I was before I got confused. Almost 20 years ago I got a call from a friend saying he needed to talk to me. Although I loved this guy, I did not necessarily consider him a paragon of Christian virtue. As it turns out, his wife had taken a shine to another guy and wanted out of the marriage. Kids, property and quite a few years together merely complicated her exit; she was gone. My job was to support my friend, so we quickly put together a time for golf, eating, and venting. As we sloshed our way through dinner, passing up few chances to villainize our new enemy, my buddy confessed his belief that this was not his wife's first affair. That observation didn't exactly startle me, but his next statement did—and it hurled a wrench into my system of ethics and virtue. Sheepishly, he peeked over his glasses and said, "But I never cheated on her." Incredulously, I asked why. "Well, I was tempted several times," he said, "but I knew it wasn't right." Here I was, the big Christian ministering to my secular friend, but I knew that if I were in his shoes, only my reverence and fear of God would have delivered me from the suspicion and vengeance that would have provided the perfect excuse to satisfy my lust. I realized that I had never constructed a personal morality independent of my faith in God.

Several years after this incident, I got hit with the second major assault on my belief that virtue came only from God. After I'd spent almost a year consulting with Phil Clement, then president of DeVry, Inc., we arranged for a long dinner at which I would give him a summary of my observations. I had found Phil to be consummately Christian in everything he did. While sitting on his management team for a year, I never saw Phil budge on his demand for the highest ethical standards in every decision we made. He had become my role model of integrity—no cracks. Toward the end of our meal together, I had to ask him to reveal the source of all this morality and commitment to his employees. "My grandfather, I guess," Phil said. "When I was a young boy, he worked for a labor union. He just always told the truth, and he always did what was right. There were no other options. I watched the way he lived." "But what about honoring and obeying God?" I asked. "Nah, I'd say it was my grandfather. I've never really given God too much thought," Phil replied.

When I say my commitment to virtue has become stronger now that it's confused, I mean that I no longer hold my original belief in the existentialism of "Eat, drink and be merry" as the only logical ethic apart from God. I find too many examples of non-faith-based morality for me to accept that there is no good apart from God. I do believe God to be the first source of everything that is good, but a fundamental awareness of what is right and wrong endows all people with certain moral responsibilities. For me personally, ethical resolve still rises from my longing for God's approval, but reinforcing that resolve is a profound awareness of my responsibility as a citizen of the human community. I believe that for others, not being a person of faith provides no excuse for moral compromise.

Leaders claiming that all this stuff should be left to philosophers and graduate students are dangerous. They duck their moral responsibilities, hiding behind the question of "Whose morality gets to be in charge?" That's not a bad question, but it's a bad shield. We should have no tolerance for people in positions of leadership with cavalier attitudes toward virtue, no matter what excuses they hide behind. Years ago I was discussing with a dear friend, who was serving as a Division I athletics director, whom he should choose as his men's basketball coach. We came to the conclusion that all things being close to equal, he should take the person with the strongest integrity. He did, and the success that followed was not restricted to the basketball court. The coach has become highly respected in his community and in college athletics. In fact, after he moved on to the next level, he and his wife were helped provide tuition for a student who no longer benefited from an athletic scholarship at the school to which my friend hired him.

Virtue in our leaders is more important now than ever. When organizations were such that leaders and members worked in more circumscribed roles, moral detours were a little easier to spot. Now that our line of sight isn't so straight, trust must replace surveillance. Leaders must rise to repair the moral disintegration making our society outrageous and absurd. Unless we discover some kind of moral fluoridation that prevents ethical cavities, our leaders must serve as our moral physicians. I believe the 21st century citizen will demand leaders whose competence and virtue can be trusted.

Contributing to the challenge of providing virtuous leadership is the enormous pressure leaders feel to produce results. Leaders of publicly held companies live and die on quarterly earnings. Even not-for-profit organizations can ill afford to make a good long-term decision if it throws the annual operating budget into the red. Red ink means red flags for donors who want to invest in a winner. I know that the intense pressure I place on myself can divert my attention from moral considerations. I commit sins of omission more than of commission, but that's not much to be proud of. Leaders need to recognize that virtue is good business. It delivers good long-term results because it inspires trust and loyalty in those we lead.

The tall influence of James MacGregor Burns both helps and hurts the case for leaders' virtue. When he says, "Leadership occurs when one or more persons engage with others in such a way that leaders and followers raise one another to higher levels of motivation and morality," he helps make the virtue point.[1] But when he excludes from his definition of leaders people who use their power nefariously, he lulls us into danger. By Burns's definition, Bill Clinton was not a leader, because he failed to raise people to higher levels of morality. I think Bill Clinton was a strong leader—despicable in his personal morality, but certainly a leader. By defining "leaders" as necessarily morally uplifting, we weaken our position to demand their virtue. I agree with Barbara Kellerman (ironically, of the James McGregor Burns Academy of Leadership at the University of Maryland) who objects to Burns's odd, albeit influential, definition of leadership.

> One problem with what is arguably a redefinition of the word "leadership" is that it separates those who are in the field from those who are outside it. Although most scholars and practitioners who are in any way associated with Leadership Studies…assume that to lead is to do right, those outside this still narrow band make no such assumption. Most folks use the word *leader* as it has always been used: to refer to those able to draw on sources of power, authority and influence to get others to fall into line. In ordinary conversations, for example, Slobodan Milosevic is referred to as the leader of the Serbs, no matter what he does…. While outside the rarified halls of academe I have yet to hear anyone call Milosevic a (Burns's term) "power wielder," I know full well that for most of us in leadership studies, the term leader simply does not apply.[2]

I think Kellerman's deliverance from the jargon of Burns and other academics better positions the average person to demand virtue from those who wish to lead.

What can the 21st century leader do to become more virtuous? I have three suggestions that have worked well for me:

1. Identify the virtues that you want to define your leadership. Trying to move in the general direction of being virtuous won't work. If you achieve anything, it will probably be little more than a feeling of self-righteousness, which is definitely not a virtue. Ask the folks you lead which virtues they most want in their leader. Read other people's lists to stimulate your thinking. In his book on virtues, Gordon B. Hinckley, president of The Church of Jesus Christ of Latter-day Saints, lists love, honesty, morality, civility, learning, forgiveness and mercy, thrift and industry, gratitude, optimism, and faith. We need to increase the frequency of our discourse on ethics and morality.

I remember a great discussion our family had on virtues. We were on a road trip from Washington to Chicago when my wife whipped out a tape of Bill Bennett's *Book of Virtues* and made the kids and me listen. Because I was still mad at Bennett for trying to kill the whole Department of Education when he served as its head, I supported the kids' demands that we break from virtue for a few tunes now and then. On one of those breaks, we happened to beam up the O.J. Simpson chase on our car radio. Somehow, the irony of virtue and O.J. coming out of the stereo in sequence stirred deep and important questions in our children. (By the way, I decided Bennett couldn't be all bad when I found out he once went on a date with Janis Joplin.) Think specifically about the virtues you want your people to be able to count on from you.

2. Commit yourself to openness. Life is filled with temptations that intensify when nobody's looking. Sometimes I have been tempted to live a bit more luxuriously on my business expense account than I would on my own money, a practice I find lacking in virtue. So I've told faculty members that they are welcome to review my expense reports if they have concerns. Sometimes, especially when I travel, I'm tempted to look at garbage on the Internet, a practice I find lacking in virtue. So I've given permission to our information technology people to look at my site-visit logs.

Sometimes we're all tempted to conceal information that we feel others can't handle or will misunderstand. Such paternalism lacks virtue, and openness is its most effective antidote. I don't consider openness to be some kind of desperate measure to save us from ourselves; it just keeps the light on. Virtue always stands up under scrutiny. There is a certain honesty belonging to those who live their lives in the light, and honesty is definitely a virtue.

3. Be honest with yourself. In Erving Goffman's *The Presentation of Self in Everyday Life*, he argues that we all have three selves: the public self, the private self, and the ideal self. I think that many times we're not honest with these three selves. We pretend to be someone we're not (the public self), we long to be someone we're not (the ideal self), and we convince ourselves we're someone we're not (the private self). Leaders easily fall prey to personal dishonesty. Too many people blow compliments in their ears.

The most important point in my own efforts to become more virtuous occurred over a yearlong period in which I came to grips with my hidden but abundant selfishness. Faced with two situations in which my public image would get battered no matter what I decided, I asked, "What would the real Bill Robinson do?" My shameful but honest answer was that he would do what would be best for his public self. I discovered I'd been so impressed with my public self that I didn't notice the rot in my private self. I had boxes of clippings that proved I was a good guy. I had seldom looked within, and when I did, I chose carefully what I wanted to see. I was long on God-talk but short on spirituality. Only when my selfishness caved in on me was I driven inward in any kind of honest way. I had dipped to the point where virtue, ironically, came within reach. It was worth the crash.

Leading from the Middle

I've tossed around terms such as "virtue," "morality," "integrity" and "ethics" without strictly defining them, as though they were interchangeable. There are certain differences among these terms, but leaders know what they mean, and they know how badly leadership needs to stand on virtue and moral courage. Our society cries out for moral leadership. Our leaders must come through as good human beings.

There is something about being among those we lead that calls forth our virtue. At close range, we are exposed. All that we are, and all that we are not, is laid bare. Being in the middle serves as both the cause and effect of our leadership strength. In their midst, people can see most clearly whether we possess the goodness to deserve their confidence. It is where they can discover if we are the same person up close as we are up front.

The end of Psalm 78 offers a beautiful statement of an ordinary person of integrity providing extraordinary leadership, "God chose David and took him from the sheep pens; from tending the sheep, he brought him to being the shepherd of his people…. And David shepherded them with integrity, and with skillful hands he led them."

Chapter 7
Driven and Rhythmic Leadership

L eading is hard work—a lot harder than just being in charge. Good leaders love the hunt. The more pressure the better. Their favorite substance in all the world is adrenaline. They'll stand on their heads to help people achieve the group's goal. They claim they have higher standards for themselves than for those they lead, and they're lying—they have high standards for all living creatures. They're always pushing themselves. They're calm in the whirlpools, and they're whirlpools in the calm, but they're seldom resting. They feed on getting the job done.

In the 21st century, leading is still hard work, and leaders still have to push themselves, but it would be a mistake for leaders to push as they have in the past. Earlier I discussed the mounting pressure created by a results-oriented culture. Leaders feel it intensely. This unforgiving results-orientation can also serve leaders as an opportunity for replenishment. Somehow, the industrial age stamped on the psyches of most workers a clock-punching mentality. When folks stepped into leadership positions they didn't exactly shed this influence. They figured that "putting in the time" qualified them to be leaders, and for the most part, they "danced with the guy that brung 'em." Well, it's time to stop dancing with that putting-in-the-time partner.

Over the years I have come to accept rhythm as one of the most powerful life forces. Nature is unhaltingly rhythmic. Nothing can stop the march of seasons, tides, birth cycles, and academic semesters. In everyday life we can attempt to harness or create rhythm, but for the most part we are carried by the flow. We can fight rhythm or work with it, but in the end rhythm prevails. The 21st century's exaltation of results, whether idolatrous or pragmatic, provides leaders an opportunity to drive and renew themselves in concert with the rhythms of life and work. I'm not sure the current judge of results ever intended to be lenient about how and when leaders push themselves, but the judge has no choice. The punch-clock of inputs got unplugged when the law of outputs was put in force. In other words, leaders can now take the liberty to do what works best, rather than what's conventional.

The most important way leaders can take advantage of this opportunity is to work in rhythm with their personal and organizational productivity cycles. I have found that the best way to keep driving without burning myself out is to show up at the right times in the right places. I've studied the movements of academic cycles, and I know when my involvement has exponential impact. Sometimes the rhythms are subtle. For example, I've noticed that the first ten days of November often crush the spirits of students on a semester calendar. They've been at school a long time without a break, and Thanksgiving vacation still feels distant. They're tired from midterms, and the darkness that ran off Daylight Savings Time taunts them with winter's imminence. These are the days when I try to eat in the dining hall, send e-mails, and have students over to the house. On the other hand, in the fourth week of September, student life is so good they don't know that I exist. It is not a time when I'll get much bang for the spend-time-with-students buck. All groups, organizations, and leaders have cycles that need to be monitored. Misreads and absences can result in problems that could be avoided.

Knowing when to show up is no more important than knowing when *not* to show up. This is where most leaders lose control of their drive. Too often, our involvement and presence act as an oil spill, wasting our fuel and making a mess of the situational ecology. But our tankers don't start and stop easily. We're directed, we have momentum, and we can navigate the shallow waters when we get to them. We go to everything. We're omnipresent. This is where dumb and dangerous join in perfect harmony. Leaders must drive themselves hard, but they need to be smart about it. Exhaustible fuel supplies need time to replenish. Excessive involvement diminishes leader impact or creates unhealthy dependency.

In addition to reading the rhythms of the organizations we lead, we need to understand our own cycles. Chuck Boppell, CEO of Sizzler Restaurants (and chair of the Whitworth College Board of Trustees), is a great leader. Everybody in the food industry respects him. As a turnaround specialist committed to justice and compassion, he's the consummate paradoxical leader, a shrewd and uncompromising analyst with a gentle touch. Chuck's personal cycles are very interesting. It would be fair to say that he shifts gears very deliberately, which is why the food companies he's been hired to run (Taco Bell, Godfather's Pizza, La Salsa, etc.) get turned around very quickly. Knowing himself, Chuck works in large blocks. He drives relentlessly, and then takes a pretty big chunk of time between jobs or between cycles within a job, to recover. Chuck's style would not work for most mortals. When he's in his work zone, nobody comes close to his productivity. (Actually, he will slam on the brakes when his wife Karlyn shouts, "Stop!" or when one of his grandchildren flashes a smile at him.) When he relaxes, he's awfully good at being a million miles from work.

Chuck Boppell's style shows how the secret of replenishment for driven leaders lies in understanding their personal and organizational rhythms. In the past 10 years, I've initiated hardly any lunch meetings—I've attended many, but I never set them up unless I'm traveling. When I'm in town, lunch is best spent for me working or working out. I eat less, I spend less, I travel less and I enjoy myself more when I don't go out for lunch. On the other hand, mid-morning coffee meetings work great for me. Because I usually do deskwork in my office at home from 5:30 to 9:30 a.m., the company and the caffeine provide a great launch into my office workday. Having observed these patterns, my assistant arranges my activities in synchrony with the rhythms of my life and job.

There is one other type of rhythm that leaders must exploit. It is the mystical rhythm of success. My wife, Bonnie, is a professional pianist/organist with an uncommon gift of musicality. She grabs the emotions of her listeners, bathes them with beauty and meaning, and then returns a little more than she took. For her, rhythm is everything, but not only the rhythm of meter and beat. She also waits longingly for the rare, mysterious musical rhythm that presents flow and ease to artists, athletes, carpenters, speakers, writers, and all who perform rhythmic tasks. I can sit in the audience and tell when this phantom guest is paying Bonnie a visit. A beautiful legato unites notes that have lost their individuality. She becomes a messenger of something exquisite. Athletes call this "being in the zone." What is very hard technically becomes so easy.

This blessing is neither "the zone" nor an out-of-body experience; it is being in rhythm with our task. As leaders, we must search diligently for every condition that triggers and perpetuates this rhythm. When we have it, in whatever area of our leadership, we need to exploit it. In the 1999-2000 school year an oratorical rhythm showed up in my speaking for almost the entire second semester. So I spoke often, taking invitations I wouldn't ordinarily accept. Then, after not giving anything remotely like a speech for a month, I discovered while speaking at a conference that I had lost my rhythm. I couldn't think of what to say, and assembling a cogent sentence proved more than I could handle.

Driven leaders crave efficiency and effectiveness. Both their productivity and their durability depend on doing the right things well. I have become convinced that driven leaders who ignore or fight the rhythms of their lives and jobs are the leaders who crash and burn. Success and longevity are the rewards for those in concert with the natural forces of the very hard work of providing leadership.

Leading from the Middle

I find replenishment and perspective when I'm close to the core of what we do. Time spent with the students and staff generally knocks me back on course. Not long ago, my board chair wanted me to shake hands on six more years at Whitworth. I had just completed my 15th year as a college president, and it was one in which I served as chairman of the Spokane Regional Chamber of Commerce board of trustees, along with co-chairing with our newly elected mayor, a huge effort designed to reduce regional poverty. Going into the year, I was pretty much hoping the college would run on autopilot. Of course, it didn't. So the thought of six more years, after one in which I ran myself into the ground, depressed me.

I knew if I were to take this on, which is what my family wanted, I would have to get back into the natural rhythm and flow of my work. I had been doing too much stopping and starting as I shifted from duty to duty. The strategy I settled on for getting back in the groove was to get back in the middle. For me this means a semester immersed in what we do. So I have virtually canceled my travel and will teach, meet with departments across campus, spend more time in the residence halls, and be directly involved in the delivery of Whitworth's heart and mind education.

I'm convinced that leaders who spend all of their time out in front lose perspective and stumble into inefficient patterns. More often than not, their throttle remains wide open, but they waste energy. Getting back into the middle of the people and mission gets them back into the currents that best carry their considerable drive. They are renewed by the mission they are called to lead.

Section Summary

It's rare that I get overwhelmed, but yesterday I did. It was my first day back after a three-month, frequently interrupted sabbatical in which I completed the first two thirds of this book. Actually, I had been on campus often during this somewhat solitary adventure, but yesterday was different; the athletes and student leaders were also back. The symbolism of our mutual return undoubtedly stirred something within me.

Before heading to my office I decided to go on a 30-minute run through campus. I'm not much for exercise that doesn't involve a ball or an enemy, but I almost enjoy lumbering around our grounds during the summer. Brilliant mums and marigolds contrast richly with the lush green grass on what has to be the most beautiful college campus in northwestern America. As I surveyed all of the summer's capital construction projects, I noticed our football, soccer and volleyball athletes were all beating the heat with early morning practices. Running around, and occasionally through, these amalgamations of sweat and joy, I began to feel an enormous sense of privilege.

I have spent all summer thinking about leading, and as many times as I've argued, "It's not just about the leader," yesterday I was reminded how deeply visceral that awareness can be. Drawn by the visual contact I had with students while I ran, I decided to wander through the dining hall during their lunch break. As I enjoyed warm reconnections with great young people, I felt a deep sense of belonging.

Sometimes I wonder if God made me for the purpose of hanging around with students. I don't know the answer to that question, but here's what I do know beyond any doubt: our students have made me a better leader than I was ever meant to be. I can supply certifiable proof that I have just what it takes to be an utterly ineffective leader. But these young people have placed before me a text of their needs and hopes that is both readable and inspiring. Accepting their invitation for me to lead them has given me worth, direction, and honor. In that sense, they have led my growth. Without words, they asked me for a standard of leadership that felt well beyond my ability to provide. Without trying, they made me do my best.

DRIVEN AND RHYTHMIC LEADERSHIP

I have suggested that the 21st century will call forth leadership that is paradoxical, secure, communicative, inspiring, virtuous and driven. All of these qualities work better at close range than from a pedestal. We must be touched by the needs and longings of those who would follow us, and ours must touch them. We must lead from the midst of our people; the very people who have entrusted us with their confidence.

REFLECTIONS:
ENOUGH IS ENOUGH

Perhaps the most liberating mindset I've developed over the years is a well formed concept of "enough." I have been freed from making career decisions based on money, my colleagues have been freed from goals that are more about pride than about good sense, my staff has been spared the pressure to work incessantly, and I don't feel as though I'm living the life of Sisyphus—daily pushing the rock up the hill. Granted, my ability to flip the enough switch hardly lightens the driving ambition that wrecks my sleep many nights, as I worry about not getting enough done the next day. I'm only good at enough on big stuff. But making peace with enough for me has simply meant knowing when to turn.

At the personal level, I have always been able to see the idiot light come on when there's been too much office and not enough kid-time; so I turn home. The process begins in taking control of my appointment book and ends up with a family excursion. The family payoff has exceeded my wildest hopes. I thank God that this is one of the few mindsets I learned from doing it pretty well, rather than by making big mistakes.

Sometimes I find that when I turn from enough, I'm pointed toward something where there is no enough, toward virtuous qualities like justice and compassion. That's good. But other times I make the turn and simply find a new area in which to repeat my errors of excess. I start roaring in a direction that requires a swift and painful intervention by my enough instinct. I'm like a rat in a maze thinking, "Banging my head against this dead end three or four times is enough; I think I'll go bang it against a different dead end." As leaders we need to be vigilant in recognizing and declaring "enough." Too many of us are slaves of the stretch, always keeping our goals slightly beyond our reach.

I'm exceedingly better at sensing enough than I am at spotting not-enough. Mentally, I'm much more of a sprinter than a distance runner. Because I'm pretty bad at seeing "not-enough," I have worked with my assistant and my direct reports to be my "not-enough" eyes. My assistant reserves preparation time before occasions that require study. My cabinet members give me good information before they solicit my involvement. Everybody I work with reminds me to slow down. Fatal mistakes are more often the result of incomplete information than inaccurate analysis. Knowing when to declare "not enough" provides vital protection from the precipitous actions leaders are so often invited to take.

Section II
Trait-Based Leadership

In the summer of 1969 I worked in a factory cutting steel. Evidently, I'd botched one of the machinist's orders, or at least that's what I assumed while he was screaming at me. After he stormed off, leaving me teary-eyed, another machinist who had witnessed the event came over and told me I had no reason to be upset. "He's Polish," my comforter explained in a heavy German brogue. "He can't help it. People are like dogs. Germans are like collies; Poles are like mongrels. They're born that way." I didn't find much comfort in his racism, but it did become clear to me that his generation and culture felt that "born that way" was a more powerful influence on behavior than socialization.

In the early years after scholars placed the suffix "-ship" on the backside of "leader," the two words were pretty tightly connected. "Leadership" referred to the traits of a leader, and "born that way" described how most folks thought about being a leader. This tight connection between "leader" and "leadership" was reinforced by a particular research methodology and a huge, extraordinarily well-organized, laboratory. The laboratory was the United States Armed Forces, perfectly arranged by rank. The research method, quite popular at the time, correlated the relationship between rank and various personal characteristics. But the military was not the only controlled environment researchers studied. Gangs and children's groups also served as leadership microcosms. Characteristics of children whom other kids voted as their leaders were interpreted as general leadership traits. This extrapolation supports the point that researchers were not yet looking at the influence of context on leadership effectiveness.

In its simplest form, this correlational research method would identify or determine the position or rank of subjects, then look at how they scored on measures such as talkativeness, humor, physical appearance, and originality. If, for example, 50 lieutenants scored significantly higher on a creativity test than 50 privates, creativity was declared a leadership trait. Hence, the variables with the most direct correlation to an advanced rank were considered leadership traits. Correlation research makes no claims about cause and effect. Its modest conclusions report that the frequency or magnitude of two positively correlated variables will rise and fall together. If a study shows, for example, that there is a "significantly positive" correlation between height and annual income, we can only conclude that the taller a person is, the more money he or she is likely to make. However, we can't say from the research that height improves earning power (or that being rich makes you taller).

Because of these limits in the research methods, the traits found among leaders in these early studies are not necessarily the cause of their leadership. They are simply the characteristics that people associated with leaders. In fact, the overwhelming conclusion of today's leadership scholars is that, "The early studies failed to support the basic premise of the trait approach that a person must possess a particular set of traits to become a successful leader. Although some traits appeared widely relevant for different kinds of leaders, these traits were neither necessary nor sufficient to ensure leadership success."[1]

As with most research efforts, the leadership characteristics found from study to study varied. It almost seems as though the principal criterion for choosing leadership subjects was their availability. However, a broad sweep of the findings suggests that the most frequently found characteristics in leaders included three traits related to effort and four traits related to personality:

Traits related to effort:
- Desire to excel
- Aggressiveness
- Energy

Traits related to personality:

- Originality
- Popularity
- Humor
- Sociability[2]

These qualities continue to facilitate leadership (although their individual favor has waxed and waned through the years), but it's interesting to note what's missing. Neither intelligence nor physical characteristics correlated as highly with being a leader as the above traits. Apparently, back then a person could attain a leadership position without having the native intelligence that our information age now exalts.[3]

In academic research, being first doesn't always get the blue ribbon. I've yet to see a research project conclusion that reports, "The initial studies hit the bull's-eye—no more research is needed. Let's move on." Granted, there's always more to be learned about a finding, but there is something to be said for our first impressions, even in the field of research. So, I do not dismiss these early studies as anachronistic or culturally outdated. I think some very good stuff came out of our first looks at leadership.[4]

In the "post-traits" periods, the qualities listed above are neither necessary in their entirety nor sufficient individually to constitute good leadership. Nevertheless, the presence of these characteristics can be very helpful in supporting effective leadership.

Chapter 8
Traits Related to Effort

I was once the guest of a U.S. Congressman at a dinner on a 147-foot yacht. The owner of the boat was hosting the transportation committee of the United States House of Representatives. Not only did this nice man own the boat, he also owned a trucking company and rather hoped that this fact would not get lost on the 15 congressional delegates who joined him for a little dinner-cruise on the Potomac.

Somehow over the course of the evening I had a chance to ask our host how he'd built such a successful company. I didn't expect him to make reference to buying off politicians, but I also didn't really expect such a basic answer. Our host simply said, "I love hard work, and I demand it from others."

It's one thing to like hard work, but this guy was foaming at the mouth on the subject. His best story was when he encountered some employees standing around at a loading dock with one of his trucks yet unloaded. As the story goes, our hard-work advocate ran up to these guys, reached into his pockets, grabbed all of his change and flung it at them. He then dipped into his wallet and started hurling greenbacks, all the time screaming, "You thieves, go ahead take all my money." Evidently, this man found little difference between laziness and theft.

Traits related to effort carry more of an overtone of virtue than traits related to personality, largely because of their perceived controllability. When I became a college president and saw such learned colleagues leading our rival schools, I thought my only chance of keeping up with these folks would be to outwork them.

It was the one thing I could control. Leaders communicate a work ethic more by example than by explanation. For this reason, it is of no surprise that early studies found three of the most recurring leadership traits were related to effort.

1. Desire to Excel

It was a normal Sunday—the day of the week I try to set aside all that rages within me to meditate on God's good grace—when a brutish desire to excel rose from my viscera and conquered my brain. I couldn't stop it from coming. This particular conquest of reason started innocently enough. As my wife was leaving to prepare for her duties as church organist, I asked, "Which service are Ben and Bailley (son and daughter) going to?" Bonnie replied that they were not going to church, but were instead participating in a "fun-run" fundraiser at Bailley's high school. For me, "fun run" is an oxymoron, so I should have kept my distance. But when Bailley, cooed, "Come on, Dad, run with us; we'll just go easy," I was hooked, as only my daughters can hook me. Although I caved in, I made a solemn covenant with myself that I would jog lazily. I even called one of Ben's friends and made him promise to run with me, just so I wouldn't try to keep up with my rabbit son, knowing he'd break his promise to go easy and would take off like a rocket.

Two minutes before the race, this blood-of-my-blood scoundrel looked at me and said, "You're not capable of going easy," then threw back his head and laughed. He was right, I was already abandoning my vows of moderation. So I spent 39 minutes and 27 seconds torturing myself, running frantically up the side of a mountain because when I stood at the starting line, a voice inside me said, "There's just no way you're taking more than 40 minutes to run this sissy course." It was about a week before I could walk without assistance.

The desire to excel can be found in the DNA of every successful leader. The self-evidence of this statement is so clear that I have chosen not to include rags-to-riches accounts of people who made their ascent using the fuel of this compulsion. Rather, I will focus on the ways in which the drive for excellence needs to be channeled. It's one thing to lose control of that desire and end up with jelly-legs from a stupid decision about a race; it's quite another to be intoxicated by the lure of achievement to the extent that strategic equilibrium and moral sensibilities are lost.

It may come as a surprise that not all the studies tracking the relationship between the achievement drive and effectiveness conclude that the more you have of the former, the more you'll have of the latter. Although much of the research on the connection between the excellence drive and success proved to be positive, some studies have actually found a negative correlation between these two variables.

Gary Yukl explains these equivocal findings by suggesting that perhaps the relationship is curvilinear—we can have too much of a good thing. Up to a certain point, the more drive you have, the more success you get. Beyond that point, your compulsion begins to undermine your success. Yukl suggests that some of the diminishing-return points might be excessive risk or conservatism, unrealistic goals and deadlines, and reluctance to delegate.[1]

I suppose perfectionism and workaholism also come along as companion viruses of those who let their desire to excel move into the danger zone.

Twenty years ago, at 3 a.m. in my living room, my dear friend Boyd Wilson, now a brilliant religion professor at Hope College, helped me see my greatest vulnerability related to the "excellence drive". Emboldened by too little sleep, I lovingly offered my opinion of his fatal flaw. There must have been a lot of love in the room, because he returned the favor. He said, "Your biggest problem is that you think you have to be better than everybody at everything." After peeling off layers of defensiveness, I began what would be one of my most important professional journeys. Slowly, painfully, failing and flailing, I became the founder and only member of my own "Winaholics Anonymous." I am still in recovery.

In one statement, my friend pointed out two desire-to-excel problems: breadth and measurement. I was in deep trouble. My breadth problem, "I must be better at everything," was keeping me from delegating. Having reached the age of 30, I'm sure I thought I was good at everything. Why sacrifice quality in the name of delegation? At the time, I was dean of a fledgling department in a college. I'd been awarded this position because the provost decided to try unleashing my hungry, win-at-all-costs compulsions on this program before deep-sixing it.

I did delegation-free administration and taught more than a full-time load. I taught because I felt I was better than the other faculty members; and I didn't charge the college for my teaching because I was obsessed with making our budget. I was going to make this thing work if it killed me, which is what it was doing. I had lost my balance, and my soul wasn't far behind.

But blessed reality came to the rescue. With the help of my friend, I realized that I'm not good at everything. In fact, I'm not good at most things. I never will be. I don't have to be. Whoever said "You can do anything if you really try" was lying. You can't. You might "want to be like Mike," but it isn't going to happen, no matter how many hours you work on your moves. Further, you'll waste a lot of time working on what *Mike* can do rather than what *you* can do. My effectiveness began to rise when I made peace with the long list of capabilities that God left off my gift list.

The breadth problem had me so busy lunging after excellence in every direction that I didn't notice that I was running on a treadmill. The term my friend used that cut the deepest—that made me realize I was chasing the unattainable—was "better." I was willing to admit my desire to excel at many things. Virtue can be found in such a desire, but my only measuring device was comparing and competing with others.

The poison of "better" is in its relativity. Its achievement depends not only on my progress but also on somebody else's. The fundamental difference between excelling and winning is the difference between an absolute standard and a relative standard. I remember when my high-school daughter's good friend traveled 800 meters in 1:53.87 in the state high school track meet. Until that day, nobody in the state that year had broken 1:54 in the event. Unfortunately, three guys in the state meet ran faster than 1:53.87, so her friend didn't win, but he did excel, and to deny that would be silly and hurtful.

I hate Vince Lombardi's statement that "Winning isn't everything, it's the only thing"—another great piece of pith from the world of sports. For those of you keeping score at home, when something becomes "everything" it becomes "only." But I do agree that winning is sweet, and can be quite noble if properly understood.

Shortly after I became the president of Manchester College, in Indiana, we had the 1964 10,000-meter Olympic Gold Medallist, Billy Mills, come to campus for our lecture series. I vividly remember watching his famous victory, alone in my house, screaming my head off. As we chatted during the afternoon of his arrival, I asked Billy what he was thinking as he mounted that famous, furious kick that gave a couple of Englishmen a good view of his backside crossing the finish line.

He told me that every night for two years he went to sleep picturing himself surging at the moment he thought he'd lost the Olympic race. He went on to say that at the final turn of the final lap, he got tangled up and tripped. The moment he stumbled, he thought to himself, "I've lost the race." And at that point he felt the surge that for two years he had imagined. Mills said to me, "Bill, when I felt the surge, I knew I'd won because I reached the goal I'd set for myself. At the time, I didn't really think I'd finish first, but I knew I'd won the race."

It is hard for me to express the liberation I have experienced having redefined "winning the race" in ways that do not depend on the success or failure of others. Our deep desires for excellence must focus on controllable elements. They must be spacious, allowing for co-workers, and even competitors, to excel as well. We share a city with Gonzaga University, our #3 cross-application school in competing for students. Everyone knows how highly I esteem Gonzaga and admire its president, a dear friend. I would bet anything that my public affection for Gonzaga has not cost us one student or one dollar. It has, however, made it clear to our community that Whitworth and Gonzaga are partners in a common goal of making Spokane a great place to go to college. We will both win.

Leading from the Middle

If there is a *sine qua non* of leadership success, it is probably the desire to excel. It is a commitment that must penetrate every corner of our organizations. It must be modeled, proclaimed and distributed. It must be crystal clear to both our customers and our employees, but this desire must also be regulated. The modeling, proclaiming and distribution of our desire to excel are not done well from a distance. They are done best when our people are in a position to see our commitment, to hear us when we speak in a normal voice, and to volunteer to join in the cause. Our commitment to excellence is communicated better when we help move the chairs around to make the room just right than when we send an e-mail to the physical-plant employees about our standards. Customers, as well, see best our insistence on excellence when we move in their midst, peppering them with questions on how we can improve.

Leading from the middle of the pack also reminds us just how good the pack is. We see the deft work of our specialists, whose knowledge of their areas underscore our reliance on their skill. Leaders are not only in a better position to empower from the middle, they are also inspired by the good work of the co-workers who support them and stand ready for more responsibility. Finally, the middle guards leaders from being preoccupied with "the other guy." Operating from the middle means that no matter what direction you look, you can't see the competition without seeing the good work of your "followers." Their efforts remind you that winning the race is more important than finishing first.

2. Aggressiveness

Clichés are bad. Sports clichés are really bad. Generally, they don't mean anything, and the ones that do don't apply to life. Yesterday I heard, "We had to suck it up because our backs were against the wall." How can you suck something up with your back against the wall? Having been involved in athletics my whole life, I have to admit that one axiom does apply in some team sports, "The best offense is a good defense." The saying does not, however, apply to leadership. There aren't too many highly successful business ventures built on playing defensively. Early researchers found aggressiveness to be a trait present in most leaders. The term "aggressiveness," as used by Bass, represents a collection of qualities such as persistence, initiative, and ambition.[2]

Too often, people in positions of leadership get bogged down playing defense. We can certainly be very aggressive in defending our organizations or ourselves, but the best leaders channel their aggressiveness toward reaching their goals. The really aggressive ones love to score. Pitchers' duels are for sissies; these leaders want to see balls flying out of the park. Deep down inside, good leaders love the hunt. It's hard to hold them back.

The 21st century, however, greeted unbridled aggressiveness in a very unfriendly manner. Wall Street punished the young dot.com turks who didn't believe there was any point of diminishing returns on aggressiveness. Every virtue taken to excess becomes a fatal weakness. The demons of excessive aggressiveness seem to leave a worse mess than, for example, too much of the originality or popularity traits.

Aggressiveness must always be practiced in a way that recognizes the tension it's creating. Aggressiveness usually narrows our vision, which is not bad—we call that focus—but it also creates tension on people, tasks, or goals that compete for its energy. Take the dot.com cowboys, for example. A whole pack of dot.comers charged relentlessly after market share, leaving behind an important companion—profitability. As it turns out, they were sprinting after fool's gold. Fundamental to every free-market system is the naturally inverse relationship between profit margin and market share. In today's economies, unless another variable comes to the rescue, big sales volume requires narrow margins, and vice versa. Jacking up our aggressiveness does not change the basic laws of economics.

Going fast is fun, and we get to our destinations sooner than if we plod along. I do like speed, but it can be dangerous. When I'm in a really aggressive mode, I'm energized and focused; that's when I'm least likely to hear voices other than the ones in my head. Recently, I set out to solve a nagging problem that was draining energy and resources from our college. I put my head down, plowed through the obstacles and got it done as quickly as possible. I also failed to hear a trusted colleague's very important questions on the matter. Looking back, by speeding through the problem I did more harm than good. I didn't recognize the tension my aggressiveness was creating.

Our organizations will fail to reach their potential without aggressiveness. Whether it be the plugging away of the tortoise or the darting of the hare, we must push hard. I try to always compliment aggressive mistakes, telling my co-workers that those are the best kind. As leaders, we need to model aggressiveness, but we absolutely must be sensitive to the tensions we're creating. Aggressive moves get us closer to our goals, but they also get us closer to breakpoints we can ill afford.

Leading from the Middle

Few leadership traits need to be "surrounded" as much as aggressiveness. Leading from the middle of the mission and the people is the safest spot for the aggressive leader. Constant contact with the mission will protect a leader from the kind of opportunism that seduces organizational jet pilots.

One could probably make the case that it was aggressiveness that made Nixon-adviser-turned-convict-turned-Christian apologist, Chuck Colson, very valuable to the president, and excessive aggressiveness that landed him in jail. When Colson got out of prison he started Prison Fellowship. In those early years, I helped out as a consultant for the program. When the organization was small, it grew by opportunity as much as by mission. As it got larger and Chuck had more opportunities, the organization went through a bit of an identity crisis. Eventually, Chuck got closer to the middle of the organization, surrounded himself with his mission-driven people, and led from there instead of from out in front. Since then, the Prison Fellowship has done well, and Chuck's aggressiveness has been focused on the things he does best.

Being in the midst of one's people also positions the aggressive leader to hear voices other than the ones rattling around in his or her head. Aggressiveness creates mistakes. A good way to test your aggressiveness quotient is by counting the number of failures you've inspired. If there aren't any failures or mistakes, don't brag about your aggressiveness.

My son is a superb skier. He isn't superb because of his great balance or strength, but because his favorite place to ski has always been on the absolute limit of his skill. For him, skiing a run and not falling means he didn't ski hard enough. If we're going to make mistakes of aggressiveness, we better have folks around us who can anticipate what we can't see; people who know us well enough to warn us and redirect us a few degrees; people who will pick us up when we fall. We need to be in a position to hear these people. A post mortem with my colleague whom I'd failed to hear, and had hurt in the process, revealed to me that I was running too fast and had traveled so far from the middle that I was deaf to his voice.

The final reason aggressiveness works best in the middle of one's mission and people is that it is from the middle that a leader's enthusiasm best rubs off on the corporate culture. I push our mission hard. Not everyone at our college agrees with what I do, but no one will deny that I'm aggressive about our mission. The mission aggressiveness that people see first-hand has helped convert a written statement into a shared set of values. James Kouzes and Barry Posner make their case for the impact of shared values in reporting a study that found companies with corporate cultures based on a foundation of shared values "outperformed other firms by a huge margin."[3]

At our last comprehensive regional accreditation visit, I greeted the team of 10 evaluators with "Let me do with you what I do with all visitors and tell you about our distinctive mission." The twenty-some people in the room from our college had to be thinking, "Here comes the broken record." But in my exit interview with the team's chair, she reported never having been at a school with such a shared sense of mission. A leader's aggressiveness will invariably be positive when leading takes place from the middle of the mission and of the people.

3. Energy

Energy is a strange force when viewed in isolation. Physicists and philosophers agree that energy has no intrinsic moral property. My dad felt differently. Two of my sixth grade friends were Rodney the hell-raiser and Danny the docile. After I'd oozed my way home following an afternoon of TV and potato chips with Danny, my dad greeted me with, "How come you haven't been hanging out with Rodney lately?" I was incredulous. Less than a month earlier, I'd arrived home from a little-league game to a chalkboard note that read, "Billy, we have gone to prayer meeting. You are to go to the police station and ask for Sergeant Pete Anderson." Grrr. It had been just a normal day with ever-restless Rodney. So, thinking my cleric father had either lost his memory or decided my best occupational bet was crime, I simply replied, "Rodney?" Dad muttered as he walked away, disgusted with his sodden son, "At least he has energy."

That's when I discovered that Dad wasn't kidding when he would bark, "Do something, even if it's wrong!"

Few of the early researchers tested energy as a correlate of leadership, but the ones who did found that most leaders tend to be endowed with an abundant reserve of energy, stamina, and ability to maintain a high rate of physical activity.[4]

I've improved at directing my energy. My assistant and the folks who report to me know that my goal is to sink most of my energy into doing only the things that only I can do. That goal is less pompous than it sounds. For example, the staff can draft a perfunctory acknowledgement from the president, but only I can help a student carry suitcases into the dorm and have her call home to say, "Guess who helped me move in?"

A good leader can create energy in the organization without always supplying it. In December of 1985, syndicated columnist Mark Shields published a column that argued Ronald Reagan had outperformed Jimmy Carter in the presidency because Reagan himself supplied less direct energy to his office. Shields used an interesting model to make his case:

> Nearly five years into his presidency, Ronald Reagan has again recast the chief executive's job, this time somewhat after a model used by the turn-of-the-century German general staff. In searching for its future commanders, the leadership of the German army put every officer into one of four groups. The first were the dumb and the lazy, who were going nowhere. Second were the dumb and the energetic (clearly the most troublesome subgroup in all organizations). Third were the bright and the energetic, who were passed over for the command assign-

ments but who were thought to make the best staff people. The command posts were to go to those in the fourth group—the bright and the lazy—who were deemed most capable of figuring out the easiest as well as the most sensible means of accomplishing an objective.[5]

Shields went on to observe, "Jimmy Carter was obviously bright and relentlessly energetic, while Ronald Reagan is bright, if less obviously so, and not given to bragging about long hours in the office." This lighthearted comparison points to the difference between a leader being the fount of energy and being the catalyst of energy.

In the utilities industry, energy is converted into power. In organizational life, power is converted into energy. Ronald Reagan delegated power, not just responsibility, and that power created energy. I believe one of the reasons the U.S. economy soared in the 1990s is because during the last half of the 1980s our country's flagship companies pushed power closer to the customer. The woman at the counter and the guy at the cash register got new jobs. They became problem-solvers and decision-makers rather than vacant bureaucrats. This movement injected energy into the heart of workers while freeing general managers to become strategists rather than high-paid operators.

I think leaders should personify energy. One of the few things in life we can totally control is our effort. I love the rush of busting my tail, whether it's at work or play. At eleven o'clock on a Saturday night I sent an e-mail to the president of the University of Washington. I can't remember what it was about, but I remember smiling when the reply came instantaneously. He was at his desk. I suspect we had both gotten home from some event and still had a little gas in our tanks. I will admit that part of our energy quotient shows up in how we feel. Some days I wake up with the zeal of a slug. But I also believe that energy is a choice that leaders must make, and the more often they choose it, the less often the slug shows up.

Leading from the Middle

The first person I ever saw lead from the middle is still my best example of what it means. I could have used him for a model for every leadership trait, but he was really good at generating energy by staying in the midst of his people. I was 22 years old when I met John Thatcher, owner and president of the company his late father started, Yes Banana Supply Inc., in Miami, Florida. John was a man of towering integrity whose lunch pail seemed to be packed with the loaves and fishes of virtue that absolutely energized his employees. John was exactly twice as old as I when we met. When I would stop by his office to say hello, or to meet him for golf, he'd deliver a ritual homily on the physical, moral, social and spiritual benefits of the banana. My, how he believed in his product! Then, on those lucky days when he didn't have a bunch in his office, we would head for the yard in pursuit of the yellow torpedoes that John believed shot right into the soul with all that is right and good.

Those walks through the yard imprinted me forever with a picture of how I wanted to lead. To me, walking around the company with John felt like a victory march. When this man, born of privilege and stationed, almost without choice, in his father's vineyard, walked back among his loaders and truck drivers, he took on hero proportions.

I could never keep myself from commenting to John about how his people all seemed so purposeful in their work. Big smiles would cross their faces as they waved, shouting, "Hey, Mr. Thatcher," while darting wherever. John would always attribute their energy and dispositions to his having hired good people. As I got to know John, I discovered it was far more than that. I worked at John's church, having compromised my commitment to spending a year as a hobo after graduating in January from a college in the tundra region of the United States.

One Sunday after church, John invited me to play golf at his country club. Having never golfed at a country club, I was slack-jawed at its opulence from the moment we arrived. So, of course, I asked John how often he golfed at this luxurious course.

"Weekend afternoons if I'm lucky," he said ruefully.

When I asked why he didn't play more often, he shrugged and said, "I don't think I should play golf when my people are working."

It was at that point I knew what put bounce in the steps of the employees at Yes Banana Supply Inc.

Leaders don't rise to their positions by sitting around the house doing their nails and drinking Pepsi. They work hard. The people they lead need to draw energy from the commitment they see in their leader. As we move into the midst of our people, the electric current becomes reciprocal. We create energy in them and they create energy in us. Leaders must realize that the lunchroom can be as great a generator as the boardroom.

REFLECTIONS:
REACTING: THE FIRST RESPONSE

Hard-driving leaders tend to keep their engines revved at very high RPM levels. They're lucky to even notice the roses that you're supposed to stop and smell. These folks are not always in the perfect frame of mind to greet difficult surprises as carefully and deliberately as they might. And whether they like it or not, everyone is watching. They're taking their cues from the leader. I've found that the first response of the person in charge to almost any situation is like an entrance to a highway express lane. You can't exit; you can't turn back; you're on your way to wherever it's going.

I've learned this rule from failed attempts to backtrack, and from a couple of successes. In December of 1995, our family set off to spend Christmas with my sister and her family in Caracas, Venezuela. A snowstorm in Chicago rerouted us through Miami, where I had lived in my single days. Taking advantage of a five-hour layover, I rented a car and decided to take my family to the beach where I hung out years back. After a 30-minute walk by the water, we returned to the car. I got there about a minute before Bonnie and the kids. What I found was a broken window and a burglarized car. Our carry-ons, the money the kids had saved, Ben's new camera, our tickets, passports, the works, all were stolen.

As the family approached the scene, somehow my anger was interrupted with the thought that our children would never forget the next five minutes, and my response to this mess would probably determine our attitudes toward all that would follow. Having that 60-second lag time gave me a chance to think, rather than to react. How I interpreted the disaster to the family bore little resemblance to the rage I felt at the moment of discovery. Somehow, I found the words and tone to communicate comfort rather than anger. I'm sure I remember my self-control because it contrasted with my usual knee-jerk emotional reactions, and because I had to control my knees a few more times trying to get passports from the federal government that had shut down.

Eventually, we made it to South America with the disaster put well behind us. As I have been faced with crises and surprises since then, I haven't forgotten the value of that lag time I used to gather myself. I have also discovered that the availability of lag time doesn't have to be controlled by circumstances. If I spend my first moments absorbing after encountering bad news, unfair accusations, horrible situations, or any big surprise, I can create a bracket of think-time before I respond. Remarkably, thinking always improves the way I deal with a situation. Which response will get us headed where I think we need to go? My brother's obnoxiously repetitive refrain from my youth—act rather than react—has turned out to be pretty good advice.

I know there are times when we botch our initial handling of difficult situations. I've sent a few ugly memos I wish I had back. Apologizing to offended parties, changing courses, and confessing our sins of overreaction are better ways to handle dumb responses than digging in to the bitter end. Sometimes we're wrong, and the odds of being wrong are greater when we don't have, or take, time to think.

Passing the 24-hour law has helped me. When I learn of a situation that angers me, any decision or response I make has to be discussed with a cabinet member, then delayed 24 hours. Besides putting my mind back in charge of my tongue, I have found that the 24-hour cooling time doesn't alter most of the situations that I thought needed my instant response.

Sometimes we get into an referee mentality. I think basketball would be improved if the referees were required to think for a couple of seconds between when they blew their whistles and when they made the call. Just think of the suspense that would build as everybody in the arena chanted, "One thousand and one, one thousand and two..." while Bob, the referee, contemplated his pending call.

Chapter 9
Traits Related to Personality

In the introduction of Chapter 8, I made the claim that traits related to effort are somewhat more controllable than traits related to personality. Someday geneticists may prove that claim to be false. It may be that aggressive, energetic people who seek excellence have an "effort gene" lighting a fire in their DNA. But originality, popularity, humor, and sociability seem to be more directly related to a person's fundamental personality than how hard the person pursues his or her goals.

It might be that personality traits would fascinate me less had I not been born in 1949. I first heard the term "charisma" in reference to John F. Kennedy. I am certain that no other time in U.S. history were sixth graders claiming that one presidential candidate was "all charisma." But in my little GOP town, JFK had too much charisma to be trusted (plus, our parents were telling us we'd be electing the pope as president). In the second half of this decade, I watched Martin Luther King Jr. rally millions of people by infusing a moral cause with his captivating personality. I am still convinced that the course of history turned in the 1960s on the strength of personality-based leadership.

It would be a mistake to think these four personality traits are indispensable elements of leadership. I see them rather as facilitators. It would also be wrong to think that "you either have them or you don't" just because they may be somewhat less controllable than traits related to effort. All four of these traits are worth developing, no matter where we start.

1. Originality

I can't say that everything I needed to know about life I learned in kindergarten, but I can say that one of my great lessons in originality took place in a kindergarten restroom. It was spring of my senior year in high school, and I had landed the job of janitor at my old elementary school. Head custodian, Dick Lau, was taking me on a tour of my duties, showing me my job description. As we were working our way down the kindergarten /1st grade hall we turned into the boy's room. I remembered it well as the one place Miss Rimshus learned her lesson to let me visit on demand.

Two steps into my old haven, I knew Dick Lau was a creative genius. Eighteen inches off the floor, painted right in the center of the white porcelain urinals, were brightly colored bull's eyes. "Yeah, Bill, back when you were a kid you guys would start peein', then some kid would give you shove or tell you to look at his rabbit's foot and you'd spin around like a lawn sprinkler. The day I painted those bull's eyes is the day I stopped cleaning pee off every wall in this room."

I don't know if I can hold this up as the kind of original leadership we need in the 21st century, but here's one guy who had to "color outside the lines" to get little boys to "pee inside the toilets."

If I never again hear the term "paradigm shift," it will be too soon. But I have to admit, no matter how tired I might be of this trendy term, it is undeniable that the 21st century will require its leaders to think in very different ways than "business as usual." Valuing originality in the way we see our tasks will unlock creativity among all with whom we work. A leader must either possess or recognize originality to survive in a relentlessly changing society. Here's an example:

Once I went to a Lowe's hardware store to buy a couple of cotter pins and nuts for the propeller shaft on our boat. I had lost the ones I removed after slamming into the side of our garage and bending the propeller. I did measure the size of the shaft, but I didn't write that down because I'm dumb enough to think that if I remembered to buy what I'd lost, I would also remember whether to get a 5/8 or 9/16 inch nut. So with great fiscal abandon, I bought two different size cotter pins and two different size nuts.

When I got to the counter with these four items and a hedge-trimmer (which I went on to wield with swashbuckling fervor, ruthlessly severing enemy branches, along with the power cord and part of my shin) the young clerk asked me if I had noticed the cost of my small items. I had not. He looked at his phone, looked at the person in line behind me, then looked at me and said, "Take a guess." I said, "Three bucks all together." "Deal," he said, and 20 seconds later I was out of there.

Naturally, neither nut was the right size, so I had to go back and try again. I breezed in the next week, assumed the most "I'm in a hurry" look I could muster, and went straight to the service counter. In a sentence I explained my situation. "No problem," said the hardware man. "Just go back there and put back the ones you bought and get yourself the right ones." I asked if I needed to go through the checkout line. "Nah, you're fine," he said.

Do you have any idea how many pre-1980 business conventions were violated in these two encounters? I can scarcely express how impressed I was that my time, the time of other customers in line, and the compensated time of employees mattered more than a potential one-dollar mistake, which might have been in their favor. Then, to top it all off, I was trusted when I returned—another time-saving device.

Somebody at Lowe's gets a gold star for original thinking. I can almost see the big shots gasping when a company leader whispers the wild new idea: "Let's build a system and culture where we trust our employees, give them some authority, and trust our customers." The audacity!

What is it that makes us believe that in a world of exponential change, we can survive without creative, original thinking? In looking at subsequent eras of leadership, you'll find that the person in a leadership position doesn't need to be the source of originality. But the person at the top of the heap (usually the president, depending on whether it's the big heap or a sub-heap) has the broadest view of the problem. When the original thinking comes from the top position-holder, it benefits from an expansive perspective as well as a certain "leader's nudge" inherent in the idea.

I use several questions to help stimulate my own original thinking.

- What is my desired ultimate outcome in this situation?
- Is my first answer really my desired outcome, or is there a greater one?
- What would I do if I were starting absolutely from scratch?
- What would I do if I had no new resources, limited resources, or unlimited resources?
- How would I think about this situation differently if I had to defend my ideas with our five-year plan?

Generally, my failures to think creatively can be traced to looking down instead of out. The other day I heard someone say that the difference between an introverted nerd and an extroverted nerd is that the introvert looks at his own shoelaces and the extrovert looks at the shoelaces of the person he's talking to. Sometimes that's about how far I lift my sights in strategic thinking. I forfeit the advantage of my position by taking short, narrow views. It's lazy thinking, and my college can't afford it from me. I may not be the most original thinker on the team, but I need to be the most original thinker that I'm capable of being.

Leading from the Middle

The questions I use to stir my creative juices are helpful, but I'm not really one who bleeds creativity. I think my greater strength is doing scenario thinking in a way that analyzes the outcomes of new ideas. That being the case, I need to rely on others for originality. The biggest advantage of leading from the middle with respect to creativity is that it is the best position from which to solicit and hear creative ideas and solutions.

At the end of every summer, my wife and I host a picnic lunch for the college's physical-plant workers, mainly to say thanks for their hard work. After lunch, the VP to whom the physical plant reports and I always ask these workers for ideas on how we can improve our campus or our operations. We give little prizes for the best ideas and make a big deal out of it. The physical plant people love it, and they always deliver great suggestions. I find that when

I get in the middle of our people, I hear very clever ideas, ones that don't seem to find their way to my office.

A few months ago I woke up to a very full day and realized I had the evening free. So I sent an e-mail to the CEO of a publicly held company in our city and asked him if after work he wanted to play nine holes of golf and grab a bite to eat. He happened to be around and we had a nice evening. On the way to the car, I asked him how many times in his two years in Spokane he'd been called by someone to just go out and goof-off. He said this was the first. "We intimidate people," he explained. I hope he was talking about our positions rather than our dispositions. Creative thinking is risky thinking. Distance and intimidation, intended or not, discourage risk. You can't encourage creativity by remote control. You can't hear innovative ideas from the pedestal. The best way to tease creativity out of your people and your customers is by standing in their midst. You're less intimidating there.

2. Popularity

My first glimpse into early 20th-century organizational life came during my junior year in a Chicagoland high school. I found out about my hometown's meatpacking industry when Mr. Beauprez made us read Upton Sinclair's, *The Jungle*. Sinclair's novel did not exactly present an "I'm OK, you're OK" work environment. I recall reading about a rather despotic supervisor who didn't even fish out the poor slob who fell into a sausage vat, figuring that the fat banker woofing down hot dogs on the corner of LaSalle and Madison would never know the difference. I became a 16 year-old vegetarian. Popularity didn't seem to matter much to "leaders" in *The Jungle*, so why would it surface as an early 20th century leadership trait?

I suspect popularity correlated with leadership in the minds of workers because of their failure to differentiate a popular leader from an effective leader. A clear definition of leadership was even more AWOL then versus now, but according to the literature in the field, workers felt the leaders seemed to be the more popular guys. (Almost all of the studies had males only as subjects.)

119

LEADING PEOPLE FROM THE MIDDLE

Few of us today would claim that a necessary connection exists between popularity and effective leadership. In athletics, effective leadership has a very quantifiable definition: wins and losses. I'm from Chicago. During the 1990s, the least popular citizen in the city was Bulls General Manager Jerry Krause. A former Bulls head coach told a friend of mine that Michael Jordan had "No lunches with Jerry Krause" written into his contract. That's unpopular. Nobody except Jerry Reinsdorf, Krause's boss, liked the guy. But the Bulls owned the NBA in the 1990s. If nothing else, Krause was effective. A decade earlier there was a Chicago businessman in a different neighborhood than Chicago Stadium named Jim Bere, CEO of Borg Warner. Everybody in the city adored the man, and Borg Warner employees were his biggest fans. Bere epitomized the popular, effective leader. Both Krause and Bere were effective, but they differed enormously in popularity.

I've heard many leaders say, "I couldn't care less how popular I am. My job is to create productivity." Personally, I don't disconnect popularity from productivity quite so easily. I think popularity is very helpful in exercising effective leadership. Certainly, trust and respect trump popularity, but being popular, especially among those whom you have been charged to lead, provides a leader with higher levels of acceptance and margin in an organization. Folks grant a little more grace for people they like. My senior year in high school, I was voted "most popular" in the yearbook sweepstakes. I knew I'd get it. I was the only kid out of the 331 seniors who had a strategy to get it. The year before, I'd been voted student body president using the same strategy. I knew the name of every human being in our school, and never once failed to say "Hi, NAME" upon encounter. I sounded like a used-car salesman on speed when a group of ten or more students walked by. I spit out names with an election-year fervor. I'm sure I was one of the worst student body presidents in school history, but my popularity undoubtedly helped me pull off a few accomplishments and probably saved me from impeachment.

I am reluctant to admit it, but I still try to be popular—not as hard as I used to, but it still matters to me. I'd love to be able to claim that I want to be liked because popularity is one of my strategic initiatives for effective leadership; but I can't. I'm just stuck with the need. I like people, and I want people to like me. Usually that helps me provide leadership, although the need can make refereeing zero-sum resolutions very painful. Having said that, I also have to admit that I'm more concerned with being liked by some folks than by others.

The expanded acceptance and margin provided by being liked serve more as bonuses than necessities. I could sit at the controls of my college and make things work okay, but I feel advantaged when students and workers actually welcome me when I show up. When I eat in the dining commons I often sit down with a table of students whom I don't know well, or don't know at all. I feel they're sincerely glad to have me join them. It's hard to overstate how much I've learned from these times listening to students. I feel the same welcome and benefit walking into the physical-plant and sparring playfully with folks there. I learn more from more people by being a relatively approachable supervisor. As far as margin is concerned, I get a few extra chits for those rare times when I need to pull rank. Certainly you get more chits from being effective than from being liked, but now and then you're faced with the kind of issue where cashing in a popularity credit works best.

Becoming a popular leader presents a bit more of a challenge than showing that big smile in your high-school yearbook. I've thought about this quite a bit. What are the keys? There probably are no keys that can substitute for transparently loving the people we work with, but it still helps to assume a certain mindset when we set foot in the workplace.

My basic advice for those who feel the need to raise their popularity quotient is so simple it's almost insulting to mention; but here it is: Try.

Think about the dedication and effort of the people you lead. Think about the honor it is to be liked by these people. Think about what you can do not only to earn their respect, but to also earn their affection. The answer will be different for all of us, but the question is worth asking: "Why should my people like me?" Then, try to be liked. You may need to drop the symbols that remind people of your exalted position. Sometimes expensive dresses, neckties and impressive titles have to be set aside. You might even spare your geography-bound employees from a recitation of your travel itinerary and all the important people you've just seen. Instead, ask a few questions about their families and jobs. Showing that you care will go a long way toward making you a popular leader.

Leading from the Middle

I think it was some automobile manufacturer that coined the slogan, "The closer you look, the better we look." I think that's true of good people. They are usually well-liked by others, "once you get to know them." We all have stories about getting to know a high-profile person and discovering, "She was really a nice person, I liked her." Early in my academic life I was leased from my college by Bell and Howell to consult full-time in one of the companies they owned. After I'd made my first presentation to a group convened by Mr. Frey, the venerated Bell and Howell chairman of the board, he walked up and startled me by saying, "You don't come across as one of those head-up-your-ass academics I expected."

I startled myself by replying, "You don't come across as the nasty son-of-a-bitch I expected." Fortunately, he found that funny, and it paved the way for me to get to know him pretty well. He was far from the square-jawed bottom-liner that employees said he was. In fact, universally, those closest to him said the better they knew him, the more they liked him. Leading from among the people allows us to be known and liked by the people we serve. That doesn't mean we have to be buddies; it just means we have the confidence in our co-workers to step out from behind our positions.

3. Humor

This is the kind of trait that reminds us that correlation tests identify only coexistence, not causality. I haven't seen too many pictures of Abraham Lincoln caught in the middle of a belly laugh, and I wouldn't call Pee Wee Herman a leader. A sense of humor doesn't create leadership, but it probably helps.

The few studies that correlate leadership with humor reveal fairly high correlation coefficients. The definitions of humor vary, but it's clear that some kind of lightheartedness can be found in most leaders. In at least one study, laughter was the activity measured as representing humor, and leaders did more laughing than group members.[1] Maybe being a leader is funny.

My primary observation about humor has little to do with jokes. The humor that best serves leaders springs from their ability to laugh at themselves. A leader who doesn't take himself or herself too seriously wears an approachability that solemn leaders might desire but have a hard time communicating. Countenance counts. We underestimate the communication value of the persona we put on. I have nine direct reports (too many unless you like the "middle") with whom I meet weekly. One of the most important things we do is laugh. We are all willing to trade stiffly efficient meetings for a few yuks.

Working with students begs for jocularity. Our language exposes the industry. Take "sophomore," for instance. The root of "moron" is preceded by the root of "sophistry," a derisive term referring to the drivel that came from the mouths of a pompous group of pseudo-intellectual Greek philosophers. Hence, the denotation of *sophomore* is something akin to a "babbling pseudo-intellectual moron," an oft times apt moniker. Sometimes I find that the only alternative to eternal discouragement is wondrous laughter. And that's not so hard because students are fun. Regularly, I cavort with them, and they with me. It reduces the distance between us.

Laughing easily not only makes leaders more approachable by humanizing them, it can also give power to our more serious messages. As I indicated in my discussion of paradoxical leadership, contrast increases impact. Early Greek theatre often juxtaposed comedy and tragedy in very powerful ways. I received an e-mail from someone who commented on the impact of this contrast in reference to the opening paragraph of my monthly newsletter that read:

> Here's my situation. I'm not on a plane. I'm sitting on the deck at our cabin. Before me a perfectly still river reflects tree-topped mountains as a rising sun delivers warmth through the cool, early morning air. Surrounded by the splendor of God's creation, one question dominates

my thoughts, "I wonder how we're doing on the general education curriculum." I need professional help.

Actually, before I started fussing, the beauty of the earth did seem to enrich my morning prayers. Among those prayers was intercession on behalf of a wonderful friend in Portland battling the return of a virulent cancer. Please pray for her.

Life is, at once, so good and so hard. I find its joys and sorrows seem to be intensifying. Maybe I'm getting more emotional as I age; or maybe Bonnie's sensitivity is rubbing off on me. I heard that she cried at the grand opening of Alton's Tire Center. Well, I hope you are having a renewing summer season. Even when we're working hard, the change of rhythm in the academic calendar refreshes us at Whitworth.

This isn't, by a long shot, great writing. But sandwiching heartbreak between lighthearted comments can be done in a way that keeps us from being maudlin without trivializing our sadness. Sometimes life is funny, sometimes it's sad. Being able to laugh and cry is just human.

I'm not going to spend many more words on the subject of humor, other than to claim that leaders lead better when they lighten up. Sometimes, laughing is the difference between a leader being perceived as approachable or aloof. I don't really want our employees to perceive me as being bogged down by the pressures of my work. It creates unnecessary anxiety in the organization. Nor do I want an air of immunity that presents me as untouchable. Like everyone else, I have a job, I have a personal life, and there is joy to be found in both.

Leading from the Middle

Certainly, the middle of the organization provides both source and welcome for a leader's levity, but additionally humor presents leaders with a pathway to the middle. Laughter's reputation as the universal language is well deserved. That same universality provides laughter with an equalizing quality that reduces the distance between and among those who burst into it. Laughter reminds us of our common humanity.

I have a friend who became athletic director at a state university. As he was getting started, the professional dance with his president seemed to be going decently, but he still felt ambiguous about whether to draw his leader more closely into the whole athletic arena. Would the president be able to bridge the gap from his world of scholars to the world of jocks? Well, in one irreverent moment he got the answer to his question. Driving to an event, my friend glanced absently at the car passing him. To his amazement, the passenger in the back seat grinned broadly as he gestured somewhat profanely, then waved like the hare blowing past the tortoise. The hare was his president, whom he then knew could handle being in the middle of university athletics.

I'm not advocating a particular type humor, nor am I suggesting a sort of reverse-obsequiousness to try to be one of the gang. What I am saying is that humor is a good way to get ourselves off our high horses. I believe firmly that all employees become marksmen when they see their leaders riding too high. Our choice is whether we climb off the horse or get shot off.

4. Sociability

I don't have too much to say about sociability, partly because I'm not sure what the researchers who identified it as a leadership trait really found, other than something they loosely called social skills. In this respect, sociability differs from popularity, which is located in the esteem of the group, and may or may not be based on social skills.

At least eight studies find a strong connection between sociability and leadership, but most of these studies were performed on children. I pay no attention to children who lead, unless they're armed. I think for the most part, the bossiest kids elbow their way into becoming the class CEO. When Rodney transferred into our sixth grade and smacked me after I questioned his mutinous suggestion that we do things his way rather than mine, I too felt he should be our new leader. I'm not going to make too many major changes in my leadership because of what researchers learned about 11-year-olds who were voted "leaders" by their gang members.

I would have skipped sociability were it not for its proximity to a dimension of social perception that seems to make a huge difference in how people think about one another. Vintage research by social psychologist Solomon Asch offers leaders a compelling identification of one influential prism through which people are perceived socially.

During the same period that leadership styles were pushing aside trait thinking, Asch conducted studies in impression formation that suggested that certain characteristics dominated the way a person's other attributes were perceived.

In one of his most famed studies, Asch took six characteristics—intelligent, skillful, industrious, determined, practical, and cautious—then placed "cold" or "warm" in the middle of the list. To one group in his experiment he gave the list of six traits with "cold" in the middle and to the other group he gave the same list but substituted "warm" for "cold". He then had members of each group describe the person with the seven characteristics. The descriptions couldn't have been more different, stirring up images that ranged from Warm Ozzie Nelson to Cold Al Capone. "Warm" and "cold" proved to be traits that sent folks down two very different perceptual paths.[2]

If we grant sociability as a leadership trait, this research suggests that we should build on a foundation of warmth. I don't think all the heat must be on the surface, but somewhere in the leader's personage there needs to be a warmth that advocates for the rest of his or her attributes. Evidently, warmth serves as a broker of grace in how we are perceived by those who make contact with us.

My problem with warmth, and with sociability in general, is the influence that situations have over my moods. I trapeze my way between charming and distant as the situational winds blow. I hate that about myself. Not ten minutes into my assistant's interview for her job, I found myself apologizing in advance for my inevitable insensitivity.

But I'm improving by doing three things:

First, I've convinced myself of the importance of being warm, even when I don't feel warm;

Second, I've convinced myself that others do not necessarily interpret my warmth as an invitation for them to ask me about my personal life, or worse, tell me about theirs;

Third, I'm trying to make situations work for me instead of against me. I slam myself into situations that melt the ice left over from whatever had thrown me into my arctic mood. Usually, a connection with students, my children, or a couple of goofy friends can whip me into shape.

In some loosely defined way, sociability surfaced as a leadership trait. At the minimum, it seems to tint the glasses people put on when looking at leaders. While it isn't the nucleus of leadership, sociability does seem to have some facilitating value to leading others.

Leading from the Middle

The principal advantage provided by the middle in the area of sociability accrues particularly to less outgoing leaders. Some people don't lead with their warmth, but they have affirming social skills that unfold as a relationship develops. They are people who truly care about others. Leaders with sociability that lies beneath the surface do well to put themselves in a position for people to see past the veneer.

REFLECTIONS:
BEYOND WORK WITH CO-WORKERS

I've had great friends my whole life. For me they are among life's most important treasures, and I am proud to be their friend. Not only do I love my friends, I need them; so I put energy into sustaining relationships with my closest friends. Maybe it is because friends are so important to me that I never seem to retract my friend antenna, even when I go to work.

Forming friendships in the organization you supervise is complicated. Six months into my first presidency, James Fisher, author of *The Power of the Presidency*, spoke at a meeting I attended on the importance of maintaining professional distance from the faculty. That afternoon we played basketball together, after which he explained to me that it was safe to play basketball with faculty members but warned me not to golf with them. "Too much time to talk," he explained.

I decided not to take Jim's advice, as much for practical reasons (we were located in a small town) as for philosophical ones. But maintaining friendships with those over whom I had responsibility forced me to think about these relationships in a very differentiated way. Boundaries separating the work-related dimensions from the other aspects of our friendships had to be clear. The importance of these distinct differentiations was both to signal to my co-workers that my personal feelings would not invade my professional judgment and to remind me that I needed the discipline of role separation in order to maintain my objectivity.

The benefits of seeing work relationships in differentiated ways have gone beyond the freedom of forming friendships. On the other side of the coin, I have been better able to hear good ideas and advice from people who just flat don't like me than if my perceptions of them were lumped into a "consider the source" attitude. I am also able to make more relaxed connections with students as they realize our relationship exists on several levels.

Having made this point, I would be quick to agree with the claim that "You can never stop being the president," but most leaders suffer from too much rather than too little distance from those whom they lead. I have found that mentally bracketing my work relationships in differentiated ways adds richness to the social side of my job and takes the fear out of being close.

Reflections:
The Answer Is the Question

How does a president stay knowledgeable about the college, show concern for the employees, ward off self-delusion, and keep from becoming a bore? Answer: by being the number-one question-asker on campus. I've worked on this for 10 years, I've improved significantly, and I'm still terrible.

My lessons on the value of maintaining an inquisitive mindset have come from "morning after" remorse. My wife, Bonnie, loves me enough to provide me with end-of-the-evening ratios of my holding forth to my asking questions whenever I get obnoxious. I begin to loathe myself during her silent period, which begins the moment we are alone and which she breaks only when I ask for the ugly results of the evening.

Getting assaulted with the truth is bad; having to ask for the assault is worse. But my periods of reform are worth the pain. I do get into an inquisitive frame of mind that invites information from others, which is far more valuable to me than listening to the dull din of what I already know.

Being a question-asker can be gimmicky if you think of it as a technique rather than an attitude. At every level, leaders need to learn and to model learning. Neither organizations nor the workers within organizations are static. Supervisors must constantly probe if they are to stay current with their people. When we ask a question, we compliment our co-workers with a metamessage that says, "You know something that I would like to learn."

Leaders need to think about customers, co-workers, and other constituents as sources of abundant information and perspective. Usually, a simple question will unlock this rich resource. A mindset of inquisitiveness benefits everyone.

Summary Of Trait-Based Leadership Findings

Leaders in the first part of this century held certain characteristics in common. Admittedly, the researchers who identified these traits often had a rather long bridge to cross in taking what they learned from children, gangs, and even the military, and applying it to leaders in general. We should not, however, dismiss their work as naïve discoveries in the adolescence of leadership studies. I find peril in distrusting the first impressions of a major research effort. The claim that most leaders have certain qualities passes the "intuition test." Undeniably, leaders who enter the race with the fundamental properties of commitment to excellence, originality, popularity, aggressiveness, humor, energy, and social sensitivity will enjoy a significant tailwind.

Although I respect their work in identifying these qualities, I do not consider these traits to be genetically determined. I will admit to predispositions that make their development more or less likely; but to assume they can be neither lost nor found contradicts our experience. These qualities serve as facilitators in the exercise of leadership. To view them as genetic breeds overconfidence for the "haves" and hopelessness for the "have-nots."

The leadership characteristics I reviewed grow and spread well in the garden of the "middle." When surrounded by co-workers in pursuit of a common goal, leaders and followers inspire the qualities in one another that propel them toward that goal. My sprints get me off kilter so easily that I become very brisk and diffident. What gets me back on course is being clocked by the loving, velvet-covered 2x4 "upside my head," delivered by some gesture or action from the wonderful people with whom I live and work. We need to stay close to each other.

Section III
Style-Based Leadership

Following our exploration of traits, let's now turn our attention to leadership styles, and look at both how a particular style works—and the circumstances when it works best.

Many classifications of leadership studies use "behaviors" to describe the thinking about leadership in the period that followed traits. There are two influences on my reason for arguing that researchers in this stage were talking about *style* more than *behaviors*. First, "style" implies a collection of behaviors related to one another in "task" or "relationship" patterns.[1] Second, I have been influenced by the work of Robert Bales, who demonstrates convincingly that leadership behaviors and leadership roles are not the sole property of the leader.[2]

Leadership theory, over the course of the last century, has shifted its epicenter of effectiveness away from what the leader wants and toward what the group needs. In the move from traits to style, this shift is subtle. A close look reveals two ways in which the centrality of the leader began to slip. First, "style" referred to a quality that was more changeable and less inherent than traits. It was thought to be context-specific and was driven by a way of thinking more than by personality. Although theorists believed that leaders possessed "preferred styles," style represented an assumable approach to management, not a characteristic that marked a person across relationships. For example, two leaders with similar levels of originality, humor, aggressiveness, and energy could find themselves at opposite ends of the democratic-autocratic style continuum.

LEADING PEOPLE FROM THE MIDDLE

Another basis for my argument that styles represent a move away from the leader and toward the led comes from a broad look at the subsequent stages. Although overlapping, the stages in leadership studies moved from traits, to styles, to certain behaviors from anyone in the group, and finally to the leader and the group engaged in mutual adaptive action toward the achievement of a common goal. I think it was the shift from traits to style that led the way for the diffusion of leadership throughout the group. Clearly, the designated leader becomes more of a cultivator than a fountain of direct leadership as we move through the century.

During this period in which scholars focused on leadership styles, researchers began to discover that the success of certain approaches to leadership was influenced heavily by situational factors. In the first college where I worked, our chief financial officer often made the claim, "A good manager can manage anything." It's possible that he was trying to convince himself, as this was his first job in education, but I think he believed his axiom. Silly me, I thought you had to know something about your product. If we define management strictly in terms of directing the execution of operations, then my friend might have been right. Situational theorists, however, would contend that whether a leader is good or not can't be determined in a vacuum. Situations exert strong influence over the effectiveness of a particular style.

The early situational researchers (pre-1960) theorized about the relationship between leaders' traits and their effectiveness. An intriguing question for all students of this connection was whether a certain kind of leader was the cause or the effect of a situation. In other words, did the situation bring out the right set of traits in a leader, or did the leader with the right set of traits get drawn into the situation? Generating such questions paved the way for the voluminous work of the situation/contingency theorists that followed.

Many researchers have theorized about how leadership style and situation interact. The majority of the studies examined the circumstances under which either a task-oriented style or a relationship-oriented style would function best.[3] For my purposes, I will focus on the way situation influences the effectiveness of the two most frequently examined style continuums: authoritarian/democratic and task(result)/relationship.

Findings

Clearly, two style perspectives dominated the research during the middle of the 20th century. Although countless styles were identified, the majority of them can find a place on one of two continuums:

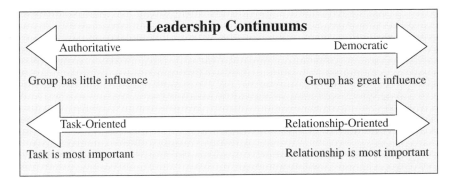

The Authoritarian-Democratic Continuum

The first, and perhaps most emotion-laden, leadership style variable is authority/democracy. How authoritarian or autocratic should a leader be for optimum productivity? This question raged during World War II, as democracy and socialism battled the forces of totalitarianism. In fact, it was a simple experiment with children that broke loose the avalanche of studies on authoritarianism that would follow. It was one of the most famed experiments in behavioral science history, and was conducted in America as Hitler was trampling Europe.

In 1939, Kurt Lewin engineered an experiment on children's playgroups from which he concluded that democracy was not only the most humane form of leadership but also the most effective.[4] The study examined how children functioned under authoritarian leaders, democratic leaders, and laissez-faire leaders. To no one's surprise, the democratic leaders accomplished the most tasks and created the best morale, while the totalitarian leaders proved ineffective and demoralizing.

Although a strong case can be made for the truth of these findings, some researchers suggested that bias crept into the experimental design. Kurt Lewin, who was Jewish, left Germany in 1933. Watching his homeland drink the poison of Hitler's brand of authoritarianism could have influenced his perspective in a way that was understandable, if not predictable. This experiment, nevertheless, was the granddaddy of a new way to look at leadership.

Throughout the 1950s, behavioral scientists studied the influence of the authoritarian/democratic leadership variable. Rensis Likert's typology represents the typical research on the continuum:

- *Authoritarian:* totally leader-centered;
- *Benevolent authoritarian:* totally leader-directed, but with consideration for the group;
- *Consultative:* leader-refereed, making the final decision after consulting with the group;
- *Participative:* leader as convener/advisor but with no more decision-making power than other group members.[5]

Parallel terms such as "teller, seller, consulter, joiner" refer to the same model.[6] Whatever nomenclature one applies, the poles remain the same with "leader-centered" at one end and "group-centered" at the other. I find it impossible to imagine that social scientists' preoccupation with democratic and autocratic leadership styles would have been as intense as it was were it not for World War II. Further, the Allied Powers' victories created an academic environment in which authoritarian styles faced overwhelming odds against coming out ahead in the comparisons with democracy.

I prefer to think of the two poles as leadership pre-dispositions or orientations. Leaders tend to drift naturally in one direction or the other. I worked at a church in which I reported to an associate pastor and he reported to the senior pastor. It would be accurate to characterize the senior pastor as leaning toward an authoritarian style of management and the associate pastor inclining to a democratic way of managing. But to say one pastor was a "teller" and the other a "joiner" narrows artificially the way each of them led. Clever differentiations, whether in leadership styles or personality types, sell very nicely but always get caught trying to force complex human beings into categories.

Task/Result-Relationship Continuum

As I mentioned earlier, I squirm a bit when I see "task/result" and "relationship" orientations on a continuum. They are not polar opposites. A leader could demonstrate both orientations or neither. For this reason I do not identify the benefits and liabilities of these two orientations in the same manner in which I present the autocratic/democratic continuum.

In practice, leaders move back and forth between task/results and relationship orientations more easily than they do between autocratic and democratic styles. It is hard to focus simultaneously on task/results and relations, and most leaders lean more naturally toward one orientation than the other.[7]

Another difficulty in discussing task/results and relations orientations emerges when attempting to look at either one, or both, in isolation. Anyone who has functioned in a leadership role has experienced the influence other variables exert over the impact of a task/results or relations emphasis. For that reason, most of the discussion to follow looks at the interaction effects between this variable and other salient influences.

In my simple definition of the task/results or relationship continuum, I put "what the group is doing" at one pole and "what the group is feeling" at the other. Results-oriented leaders place great value on completing the task. Relations-oriented leaders place great value on how group members feel about the experience. It is important, however, to bear in mind the difference between "orientation" and "effectiveness." We avoid socially oriented people who are socially inept, and we reassign, or eventually fire, task-oriented people who lack the skills to accomplish their tasks. Task/results and relations orientations refer to leaders' predominant concerns, not to their skill levels.

Chapter 10
Authoritarian Leadership

I learned a great deal about how Authoritarian leadership works during my presidencies at two different colleges.

At the first college, I was the fourth president in 75 years. My predecessor had run things for 30 years and was clearly authoritarian. Although he did take into consideration how the campus community would receive his decisions, he didn't lose a lot of sleep over making a decision that nobody liked. Every nuance of his persona declared "I'm in charge." I would have killed for his voice. His "pass the salt and pepper" thundered through the room, causing all souls present to hope they might be the bearers of that salt and pepper. You wanted to stand and salute. I, on the other hand, arrived on the scene at age 36 feeling, by comparison, pimply and adolescent. When I gave orders and barked, "and I mean it!" somebody would yawn and pass me the salt and pepper.

In my second presidency, I was the fourth president in seven years, if you counted two interims. My predecessor had very successfully led another college for 11 years and made wise, albeit difficult, moves in this, his second presidency. But reports were that he'd withdrawn somewhat on a campus that was already quite decentralized in its governance and administration. It couldn't have been a more different situation than what had awaited me at my first presidency. Interestingly, this president also fit into the authoritarian classification, demonstrating the varying effects of mixing style with a leader's traits or with a particular situation.

For example, my first predecessor involved himself directly in all the hiring and firing, personally making the offers or handing out the pink slips. My second predecessor gave his vice-presidents orders, but did not involve himself directly with hiring and firing. Both leaders functioned in relatively autocratic ways, but they differed greatly in executing their decisions.

Although the authoritarian approach occupies the cellar of my favorite styles, history isn't as harsh with some authoritarian leaders. Style stands independent of the morality, wisdom, and importance of a leader's goals. By today's standards, almost all leaders of past eras functioned very autocratically. When I was growing up, my mother differentiated ancient Israel's good kings from the bad ones by their motives. I never thought to ask her whether Jeroboam donned a more participatory style than that rascal Rehoboam. Kings were kings. They were all autocrats.

I believe authoritarianism should refer only to a unilateral style, not to motive or intent (i.e. "benevolent").[1] As a style, this continuum should be based on the degree to which the people-at-large are involved in significant decisions. I think the entire human relations movement (McGregor, Argyris, Blake and Mouton, and others), adored theories on participatory management, and put in a bad word for authoritarianism. Failing to distinguish between style and intent makes it difficult to look at authoritarianism objectively.

I am not by a long shot authoritarian in the way I lead, but I do not find the style necessarily bulging with self-interest. Although history is littered with egomaniacal political dictators, we also find those father-figure leaders who shepherd their people to safety, then turn to battle the wolves alone. Neither approach is very smart, in my opinion, but the latter abandons self-interest, authoritatively blocking followers' involvement. If we define "authoritarian" in a way that necessarily includes "lording" or "punishing," as did some researchers, then to conclude that authoritarianism is a bad style is tautological.

Four Benefits of the Authoritarian Style

I see four major benefits of the authoritarian style:

140

Efficiency. An authoritarian leadership style usually functions at a higher level of efficiency than a democratic approach. I work in an industry that has this thing called "shared governance," which means the faculty gets to weigh in on relevant matters—i.e. all matters. Most presidents consider this "faculty buy-in" the bane of their existence. Actually, I don't mind it, but it is slow. Robert Siever of Stamats, Inc., likes to quote *Fortune* magazine on what I do for a living: "The CEO isn't free to run the business; he or she needs the workers' approval for most major decisions. The pressures of managing-by-compromise force most bosses to depart within four years. As Thomas Hobbes, the 17th-century English philosopher put it, their lives are nasty, brutish, and short. Welcome to the byzantine business of higher education." Authoritarian leaders don't need votes, permission, or advice. They make up their minds and march.

Clarity. Authoritarianism takes the finger pointing out of organizational "Who done it?" The leader is who done it; now deal with it. A few years ago, our campus was squirming over problems related to freshman initiation. For 80 percent of the students, it represented a valued, sacrosanct tradition. The other 20 percent were still processing why they would be welcomed to a Presbyterian college by being immersed (not sprinkled in true Presbyterian fashion) in slime and other foreign matter. I decided to kill the practice unilaterally. I wasn't going to check with student government, our student life staff, or Mac Hall—where initiation had been lifted to an art form. I didn't avoid those groups out of fear of resistance; rather, I wanted to protect them from being accused by the 80 percent of "selling out." Unfortunately, I got conned into giving the students "one last chance" at propriety. The following year was all peace and light, but eventually the slime returned and initiation was sentenced to death democratically, evoking all the multi-directional blaming that could have been avoided had I not chickened out the first time.

Predictability. I confess to a certain annoyance with ideologues. I seem to have some dark need to profane their well-rehearsed creeds, even when I think they are right. What I like about them, however, is that they don't cast too many surprise votes. Predictability, if not taken to the extreme, has some value.

The collective trust and coherence of any organization relies on the consistency of its leaders. When determining the basic directions, goals, and strategies of a group, if leadership is centralized in a single authoritarian person, predictability rises.

Perspective. Like most presidents, I can claim that every person who reports to me has greater expertise in his or her area than I do. However, what none of them has is the breadth of my perspective. I love Max DePree's metaphor of the leader as a jazz band conductor.[2] In addition to all the specific ways in which a jazz band conductor allows the musicians to shine, the metaphor also points to perspective. It is the responsibility of the conductor to blend parts into a whole, unified sound. Authoritarian leaders find themselves in strong positions to identify discordant activity. Beautiful work loses its value if it isn't harmonized with the organization as a whole. Organizations disintegrate when no one keeps an eye on the big picture. Authoritarian leaders seldom allow that to happen.

Authoritarian leaders can provide an antidote to the stress-arousing levels of ambiguity that often characterize organizations attempting to make changes in their goals or strategies. When leadership is highly decentralized, different units can find themselves marching in different directions at a different pace. Further, the odds increase that members of the units will stick their heads over the fence and whine about "how good you guys have it" over in the pasture of that other unit. Although it is safe to say that many, I suspect too many, authoritarian leaders are set in their ways—were that not the case, they wouldn't get nervous about distributing their authority to others—they probably create less ambiguous environments. When their ways are good ways, reliable patterns bring continuity to the organization.

Four Liabilities of Authoritarian Leadership

Of course, authoritarian leadership has a definite downside. Among the liabilities are these four:

Tunnel vision. Leaders who keep only their own counsel can lose the ability to see both threats to and opportunities for their organizations. In his famed study on the danger of consensus, Irving Janis makes the argument that gigantic national blunders can be traced to "groupthink."[3] Janis argues convincingly that when a group banishes dissent, classifying it as "naysaying", bad decisions follow.

Authoritarian leadership discourages dissent. When protests have no efficacy, there won't be too many volunteers to don the prophetic mantle. But not only is defense weakened by tunnel vision, advancement opportunities are lost to the silence of the front lines.

I have a friend who made millions of dollars because the man for whom she was secretary believed that neither she nor most others in the company were capable of coming up with a good idea. Well, she was. So the company she started with one other "dumb" employee made a ton of money that could have fattened the bank account of her authoritarian boss.

Loss of ownership. Probably the most obvious loss an organization feels under authoritarian leadership is investment. Top-down leadership can allow the "downs" to feel automated. They just drive, lacking the excitement they might feel had they been given a voice in planning the trip.

My wife and I were members of a church in which the combustion of our pastor's disposition and theology fired into a strident autocracy. It was pretty much "my way or the highway." While trying to explain to the church's highest-ranking lay leader why we were leaving, it struck me. We weren't in *our* church; we were in *his* church. With no buy-in we decided to check out.

To the extent leaders depend on charges to implement organizational strategies, they will benefit from engaging those charges in the planning process. This involvement not only generates good ideas, but it inspires people to succeed. It acknowledges the leader's recognition and respect of their role as stakeholders.

Less innovative thinking. I had an amazing experience one weekend. Three guys who worked with me when I ran a camp in the late 1970s came out to Washington for a weekend. It was the first time that the three of us had been together since our camp days. As we sat around the dinner table embellishing the past, I recalled an all-camp simulation of the 1976 Olympics that turned out to be a great success.

One of the guys, now an oral surgeon, said, "What I remember most is when you called us in to help you figure out how to score events." He told about an idea he offered to which I apparently replied, "That's a great idea. You don't make very many suggestions, but when you do, they're really good." He went on to say that even now (when shyness tries to keep him silent), he has whispered to himself the liturgy of that incident.

Leaders cultivate innovation by building an environment that exalts creative thinking. Praising the thinker and implementing an idea ignites the chain reaction of ideas that freshens and improves the way we do business. When the authoritarian leader gives the impression, either real or imagined, that the "suggestion box" is unlocked only on insignificant occasions, both the box and the organization will rust. An authoritarian style can reduce workers to operators rather than thinkers.

Loss of motivation. In authoritarian-based organizations, motivation tends to be more external to the worker than in decentralized authority situations. Authoritarian leaders shoulder more responsibility for success and failure than in organizations where power is diffused. The motivation in enterprises with top-heavy authority often centers around pleasing the hierarchy, rather than in proving one's self.

Forty years ago, Herbert Kilmann published an excellent typology for understanding the motivational source of people's attitudes. A person can be persuaded (or motivated) out of compliance, identification, or internalization. Compliance refers to any power-based influence one person has over another. Identification is based on the attractiveness of, or the desire to please, the source of influence. Internalization occurs when a person believes in the substance of the influence, independent of the source's power or attractiveness.[4]

A corporate culture shaped by authoritarian leadership allows group members to function largely out of compliance. The absence of choice creates willing victims rather than enthusiastic contributors. When the authority is attractive or comes up with great ideas that the people truly believe, it is more a bonus than a necessity. If compliance is the baseline motivation, people will continue to march even if they don't like the authority or if the orders don't make sense to them. Such motivation robs individuals and organizations of the enthusiasm that results from people being able to choose the course that they believe is best. Authoritarian leadership can easily lead to compliance-based motivation.

Four Situations

Authoritarian leadership works best in four situations:

When fast action is needed. Twenty years ago, I was discussing leadership styles in a graduate course I was teaching. At the time, I leaned toward the point of view that authoritarian leadership always demoralized those being led. Faking openness, I asked if any class members could identify situations in which the authoritarian style worked best.

A class member raised his hand and began his response with, "I'm a firefighter." I knew he had me.

In crisis situations, where quick decisive action is needed, an authoritarian style will outperform a more democratic approach. Sometimes we need action that is 90 percent fast and 90 percent accurate more than 50 percent fast and 100 percent accurate. To return to the firefighting model, if there are 10 ways to put out the fire and the leader barks out what happens to be the second-best strategy, going ahead with #2 will produce a better result than having a committee meeting in order to find #1 and make sure each firefighter feels ownership of the decision.

In some decisions, speed trumps perfection. The trick in these situations is making sure the most knowledgeable person serves as or informs the leader.

When the leader is clearly the expert. Some very interesting leadership models are springing up in 21st century high technology start-up companies. I have a couple of friends who developed technologies then assembled organizations around their inventions. These young and hungry entrepreneurs disdain convention. They are in a race that offers a prize only for first place. Start-up company leaders are usually the world's foremost, and sometimes only, authorities on their technology. They become friendly, frenetic, fun-loving dictators in their tiny companies. They are the experts, and democratic gestures waste time and energy. Burn rate is their hourglass, and it's an unforgiving timer.

Certainly, as their companies grow, their need for expertise will extend to capital acquisition, marketing, finance, and all areas related to commercialization and growth. At that point these leaders will discover the difficulty of attracting expertise into a corporate culture of central authority. But for now, the founders are the experts and they aren't scheduling too many company seminars on "helping employees self-actualize through empowerment."

In some organizations, the leader never stops being the expert, and from that base an authoritarian style has a pretty long shelf life. But in an era of increasing job-hopping, leaders new to their organizations will have to depend on others for expertise on products and customer bases. The few interlopers who will be able to get away with authoritarian leadership styles will be the turn-around experts who understand the industry and how to perform organizational surgery.

When the big-picture is needed. Occasions emerge during the life of an organization when the individual units find themselves locked in a series of zero-sum relationships. In times of retrenchment, often the only way the resources of one unit can be strengthened is by reducing those of another. It is asking an awful lot of managers to strip themselves of all biases and determine what's best for the good of the whole. Armed with the strategic plan and a clear commitment to the mission, the authoritarian leader will make good-of-the-organization decisions, and in the process will emasculate the political maneuverings that these situations frequently create.

When focus is under threat. I don't know of two more formidable enemies of focus than prosperity and chaos. Both prosperity, blowing seductively in the organization's ear, and chaos, screaming epithets at the organization's gate, make it hard to pay attention.

At the moment, I consider prosperity to be the biggest threat to the college I lead. It can undermine the urgency of our workforce while it tries to convince me that I can go ahead and concentrate on tasks other than the ones that helped create the prosperity.

Chaos, or what seem to be catastrophic problems, can also attack a leader's focus. I'm on the board of an organization that found itself in disarray. Its environment had changed, and the organization had not. We hired a new president who strolled into the situation with a positive attitude, a scalpel, and an admittedly authoritarian style. His first task was to listen to what everyone had to say. Next, he clarified the focus of the organization. Having completed those two steps, he passed out marching orders and pink slips. Focus returned, and the organization is in good shape.

I'm sure my objectivity is suspect in examining the authoritarian style of leadership. I don't particularly like it, and I wouldn't be very good at it. But I do believe certain situations call for it.

I won't be completely shocked if the authoritarian style makes a big comeback in the early 21st century. As relativism seeps into every pore of our society, we will long for strong voices. Neither businesses nor individual lives will draw much direction from "I said 'maybe,' and I mean it!" Should this resurgence of authority-based leadership occur, we will undoubtedly face a different set of threats than those created by current "distributed" authority styles.

It will be interesting to see what form the authoritarianism takes, as well as how people react to it. But one thing I promise: The new authoritarians won't get away with offers to provide total direction in exchange for all of the freedoms that have been given in recent years. Nobody will make that trade.

Leading from the Middle

Leaders who function with an authoritarian style, whether because of their situation or their personality, need the middle. Because they have not heard the cheers and protests that rise from a democratic process, it is imperative that they be in a position to see how their decisions affect the people charged with implementing these decisions.

In my judgment, no United States president has blended authoritarianism and the middle better than Harry Truman. This man disdained (and often cursed) the pedestal. He stood among the American people and virtually said, "This is who I am, you decide if you want to elect me, but I will call the shots." He was legendary for calling the shots and he was legendary for standing in the middle. This was Harry. After he left the presidency and visited what is now the Truman Presidential Museum and Library, he was known to give tours, answer the phone and simply show up among the people. Harry Truman didn't convene too many focus groups to get advice or commission too many entourages to impress people. He stood in the middle and gave orders. Whether we loved or hated his decisions, that was the essence of President Harry S. Truman.

Chapter 11
Democratic Leadership

I heard a story, perhaps a fable, about one of Carl Sandburg's final public appearances. Back in his hometown of Galesburg, Illinois, Sandburg ended a speech at Knox College to deafening applause and shouts of "Encore!" He shuffled back to center stage and whispered, "Everybody is smarter than anybody," then departed. That, it seems to me, is the basis of democratic leadership.

Democratic leadership wears many faces and is perceived in many ways. Fans of the style venerate participative leadership by canting, "people matter most." Cynics of democratic leadership deride it as "the animals running the zoo." Personally, I have found that my decisions usually improve when I get input from those who will be affected. Sometimes the substance of the perspectives strengthens the decision; other times the process of discussing the decision helps me clarify its dimensions. The occasion is very rare when I'm not thankful I involved other people in making a significant decision.

Defining a democratic style can be slippery, but it is crucial to understand what it means to lead democratically. Leadership theorists from the 1950s to the present distinguish between a consultative process and a joint process. Yukl defines the former as one in which "the manager asks other people for their opinions and ideas, then makes the decision alone after seriously considering their suggestions." A joint decision, he observes, is one where "the manager meets with others to discuss the problem and make a decision together; the manager has no more influence over the final decision than any other participant."[1] This distinction is somewhat limiting because it forces "joint process" to mean one in which majority rules. A more important differentiation for me is the one between a democratic style and a democratic outcome.

Several years ago our commencement exercises outgrew the venue that had been used for years. Either the impact of enlarged, blended families or the skyrocketing awareness of just how much fun can be found in two hours and 45 minutes of pomp and circumstance fattened our attendance to an unmanageable number.

At a president's cabinet meeting we boiled our options down to two alternatives. With no clear majority position emerging, we decided to poll ourselves. The outcome was five to four in favor of option 1. I was in the "four" group, but pretty sure that option 2 was the way to go. So, in what was an unusual act for me, I smiled and announced, "the 'fours' have it." Everyone laughed, we chatted about it more to make certain we could all live with option 2, and then we moved on to the next agenda item.

This example represents a situation in which the process was democratic, even if the outcome was not. Perhaps the style would have been more democratic if I had announced that the "'fives' have it." But the process was very participatory, and either way, I am held accountable for the outcome of the decision, whether I "consult" or "join."

Incidentally, two weeks later the cabinet members returned to report that the next level of the democratic process overwhelmingly supported option 1, and that if I knew what was good for me, I would too. "The 'fives' have it," I proclaimed boldly, and we were spared a bad decision. Clearly, the masses had outperformed the president on this one.

In the following discussion, the definition of "democratic" revolves around the process of the leader actively engaging the group, and "style" refers to an orientation, not a series of steps. In leadership literature, we find a distinction between democratic leadership and participative leadership.[2] Democratic leadership refers to an organization's general information flow and power distribution, while participative leadership deals with the way in which decisions are made. Clearly, participatory decision-making lies at the heart of the democratic style, so I've chosen not to treat it separately.

Benefits of a Democratic Style

The democratic style of leadership has six benefits:

Consonance. In America, rah-rah attitudes toward a "democratic" anything have not been restricted to the post-World War II era. This is the "land of the free." We elect our leaders, and then throw the bums out if they flex their muscles a few too many times. We limit the powers of our president. We, the people, govern ourselves. So we can start with the premise that our democratic society has rubbed off on the general corporate culture of American organizations. Most workers will feel a certain consonance with a democratic leadership style.

Even as a little boy listening to "Sixteen Tons," I shuttered at the totalitarianism implicit in Tennessee Ernie Ford's rueful groan, "I sold my soul to the company store." Having a voice lives in American hearts as an inalienable right—losing it when we join a group feels somewhere between disempowering and unjust.

Trust. The idealizing of democratic styles in the field of leadership was propelled by MacGregor's famed "theory X, theory Y" proposition.[3] Theory X leaders assumed workers to be disinclined toward hard work and require some form of external incentive to accomplish their tasks. Theory Y leaders assumed that workers possessed an inner drive to be productive that could be unlocked through trust and support. These two assumptions determined what kind of style a leader would use in accomplishing tasks through others.

MacGregor may or may not have hit the target on what motivates a particular leadership orientation, but he was right about one thing: trust works. After a severe case of occupational aimlessness prompted me to drop out of Princeton Seminary, I went to work in downtown Chicago. My dad, who also worked in the city, rode a train that I could catch if I left work 15 minutes early. After a few days on the job, I mustered up the courage to ask my boss if I could slide out before quitting time.

He responded by saying, "sure, your hours are 'produce.'" Two waves of his trust washed over me in that one statement. He trusted my integrity, and he trusted my competence. I did not disappoint him.

LEADING PEOPLE FROM THE MIDDLE

Good morale. A number of studies cite findings supporting the belief that morale is higher in groups led by democratic leaders than in those led by authoritarian types.[4] Certainly to the extent that democratic leadership builds on and communicates trust, morale will rise. But there are other morale-building outcomes of this style. In basketball, telegraphing a pass hurts the team. It allows the defender to anticipate. In organizations, telegraphing a pass almost always helps the team. It allows co-workers to prepare.

People benefit from an ability to see clearly how, where and when organizational moves occur. Any leaders doubting the validity of this claim need only to tally up the times they wish they'd consulted more people on a decision and then compare the length of that list with the number of occasions in which they wish fewer people had been involved in a decision. In most organizations, morale is inversely related to the number of surprises. A democratically led environment necessarily engages people in the goals, directions, and strategies of the organization in ways that lift both anticipation and morale.

Improved decisions. It drives me crazy when a stealth cold call sneaks its way to my phone and a salesperson asks me to consider buying some office item. Other than batteries for my Dictaphone, I can't think of one equipment purchase in which I would have adequate information to make the decision. I rely on co-workers to inform me on almost every decision I make. Leaders need good information. A democratic culture encourages the free flow of information better than the top-down slopes. Something very insidious can happen to leaders when they move into positions of authority. Generally, people gain positions of responsibility because they make good decisions. Once in the positions, these same people run the risk of thinking decisions are good because they make them. I'm a huge believer in instinct, but instincts with information hit the target more times than naked intuition. Democracies arm leaders with better information than autocracies.

Improved problem-solving. Research in the field of group dynamics presents evidence that on non-complex problems individuals outperform groups.[5] On complex problems, groups do better than individuals. It's axiomatic that looking at a complex problem

152

from many perspectives will result in deeper understanding and more potential solutions than can be seen from any single vantage point. Democracies, by definition, multiply the perspectives on the issues brought before the people. Generally, complex problems beg for the breadth that only a group can bring. In complex business environments, democracies have the upper hand on autocracies.

Support. Back in the good old days, clever and loyal employees would scheme ways to plant an idea in the boss's head, knowing that implementation was dependent on him or her coming up with the idea. How the world has changed. Now the boss dangles ideas in front of the employees, hoping they'll take the bait and "own" the idea, knowing that implementation is dependent upon them. Regardless of who engages whom, the odds of putting wheels on an idea rise when the implementers participate in the decision-making process.

I have a friend who became a college president. He had perfected a style I would characterize as "leading by proclamation." I think he felt participatory decision-making cluttered his genius. All it took was a couple of bad unilateral decisions, and the faculty handed him his lunch while the trustees showed him the door.

Clearly, implementation support rises when group members participate in the idea stage. Even if the deal goes sideways, the diffusion of ownership affords the leader some support born out of a "we're in this together" attitude.

Disadvantages of a Democratic Style

The democratic style also has certain drawbacks:

Futility. The assignment given to me by our board of trustees takes the possibility of true democracy out of my hands. If my board chair were to ask, for example, "Bill, what were you thinking when you decided to allow alcohol in the dorms?" and I say, "I got out-voted," I'm history. The board has declared me a majority. So when I champion a democratic process that turns in a direction I can't support, I am immediately accused of staging a charade.

"Why bother asking us if you're not going to take our advice?" is a question I have heard on more than one occasion. My democratic pattern of getting input creates frustration when I have to make a decision that runs counter to popular opinion. What folks don't always understand is that their input invariably improves my decision, even if it's not the one they would have made.

I find it both morally and strategically wrong to ask for advice if I have already made a decision. That doesn't mean I ram decisions down people's throats, but it's never right to fake democracy. When leaders employ "consulting" as a ruse for "selling" in order to get buy-in, they don't deserve to be trusted. Even when the solicitation of ideas is authentic, the migraines kick in when the wide input that comes back is deeply divided. Inevitably, a sense of futility settles on those who counseled to no avail.

Pace. For three years in the early 1980s, I developed and sold cohort-based curricula to colleges and universities around the country. After being invited by institutions to make a proposal, I did market analyses, met with presidents, talked to deans and faculties, and then made my proposals. I'll never forget the first Catholic college I contracted. In the initial meeting, I met with the president and chief financial officer.

When I asked them about meeting with all the other groups on campus, they told me, "Don't bother." So I never did. These two guys made all the decisions. I don't know if their authority had anything to do with the school being Catholic, but the power of the president felt papal in comparison to most colleges. It was by far the fastest contract I ever put together.

Without question, the whole program, both curriculum and contract, would have been improved through a democratic process, but it would have added a year. Evidently, the two decision-makers didn't feel they could afford the time that a more democratic style would have required. Democratic processes produce good outcomes, but they don't win many ribbons for speed.

Campaigning. Democratic leadership encourages two types of campaigning. First, people attempt to exercise horizontal influence, believing their potential for vertical influence gains strength with numbers. Communication networks go into high gear when an issue is in play. Gathering allies gets rewarded when group members can influence the outcome of a decision. Campaigning consumes organizational energy and threatens productivity, especially when the lines are lit up over ancillary issues.

A second kind of campaigning sometimes contaminates the democratic process. When every issue becomes a mule to carry forward some person's or department's imperishable agenda, it's hard to get a true read on the issue at hand. In some cases, these recurrent campaigns are both noble and work-related, but they bias the process by inserting secondary concerns. Other times, issues are examined through the lens of some personal agenda.

For this reason, I think leaders with a democratic style need to exercise special caution in making sure not to hire people with agendas that run out in front of the organization's mission. The purpose of an organization is to meet a designated set of mutual needs, not to provide platforms for our favorite "-isms."

Inviting. The democratic style of leadership issues invitations indiscriminately. I sometimes brag to myself about how approachable people find me. I also sometimes loathe myself for maintaining an image that invites people to advise me on everything from soup to nuts. (Lest you think me cliché, I have in my possession an old complaint about the soup in our dining commons, and I have another note observing that one of our erstwhile employees was "nuts.") The democratically oriented leaders implicitly welcome people to weigh in on all issues, not just the ones they place on the ballot.

Living my life as a magnet for opinions, suggestions and critiques (a faculty specialty) might be the hardest part of my work. The folks who report to me sympathize and wail their litanies, "Why would they ask you?" or "It's none of their business!" or "Tell him to get a life." But you can't stand in the midst of your people and proclaim with great passion, "I want your input, but not on the stuff where I don't want your input." For a democratic leader, every day is the second Tuesday in November.

Conditions that Favor Democratic Leadership

Democratic leadership works best under four conditions:

When productivity depends on creativity. During 1985/86 I worked as a fulltime consultant to the president of DeVry, Incorporated. In the for-profit sector, DeVry held the top spot in college-level technical training, largely through establishing the quality of its products and the well-being of its people as its highest corporate values. Phil Clement, the president, had no peer when it came to engaging employees. His leadership style was extraordinarily democratic in process, although far more consultative than acquiescent when it came time for a decision. Phil never failed to till those with information or perspectives related to significant decisions, but neither do I remember him concluding a discussion with, "Well, y'all, let's take a vote."

When DeVry's research team reported that we had pretty much penetrated our target markets, Phil knew that growth depended on innovation. We needed to supercharge the corporate culture with premiums for creativity. Phil launched an innovation campaign within the organization that culminated in a daylong process at the local Hyatt Hotel. We virtually closed the corporate offices and brought every employee into creativity capsules that spun off ideas as fast as they could be recorded. Phil facilitated the whole day himself. He embodied the value DeVry placed on the ideas of its people. Phil's stubborn demand that company leaders listen to the workforce paid off when several hundred employees gave him their best thinking because they knew it mattered. Phil Clement believed that everybody is more creative than anybody, and his democratic style helped the "everybody" to believe that as well.

When decision-making depends on group members' information and support. I suppose this is a rather self-evident claim, but flashes of paternalism can draw leaders into a "father knows best" mentality, when father doesn't know squat compared to the rest of the family. Some decisions beg for group member participation.

Gary Yukl provides an excellent summary of the "information-acceptance" conditions that call for democratic decision-making: (1) when the decision is important and subordinates possess relevant information lacked by the leader; (2) when the decision problem is unstructured and the leader does not possess the necessary information and expertise to make a good decision; (3) when decision acceptance is important and subordinates are unlikely to accept an autocratic decision; (4) when decision acceptance is important and subordinates are likely to disagree among themselves about the best solution to an important problem; and (5) when decision quality is not important but acceptance is critical and unlikely to result from an autocratic decision.

I wish I had thought about these conditions before making the most important decision of the first year in my presidential career. After a very careful analysis, I calculated exactly the way our organization needed to downsize. Unfortunately, this high-quality decision of mine got trampled when it hit the street. My massive process error wasn't so much an act of autocracy as it was of being democratic with the wrong group. I conferred with the unit leaders, but I left out the department heads whose acceptance was critical to the implementation. The substance of the decision was on target, but I'm lucky I survived the mess I made of the process.

When internal motivation is needed for productivity. A few years ago, I received a call from a faculty member at a wonderful, small school. This person expressed great concern over the way the president's heavy-handed rule seemed to be launching top-notch faculty members into greener pastures. The school didn't pay very well, but the mission was inspiring and historically a climate of mutual appreciation held folks together. But the climate had changed. Whether intended or not, the president was coming across as disdainful of faculty opinions, suggestions, or anything short of obsequious worship when a decision was handed down. So the talent was leaving. If they were going to get disrespected, it was going to be for more money.

Motivation for people to affiliate with groups grows out of some combination of two rewards: instrumental and consummatory rewards. "Instrumental rewards" refers to the capacity for the group to act as an instrument in achieving a person's goals. "Consummatory rewards" refers to the pure fulfillment that comes from being a part of the group.

Two of our children illustrate the difference well. Soon after graduating from college, our freshly degreed oldest daughter conducted a job search. She has a heart the size of Wisconsin and was looking to join a church staff where she could serve people, God, and strays of all species. She had a few great opportunities, but passed them by until she found the one satisfying her principal criterion: being appreciated and mentored by the pastor. Our college-sophomore son also looked for a summer job. He too had one criterion: cash. He would remove asbestos from nuclear waste containers if the price were right. Group hugs didn't rank too high on this kid's list.

People who participate in groups largely for consummatory reasons need leaders who will engage them. These people value inclusion, the kind of inclusion that democratic styles of leadership create.

When group member stakes are high. Shortly after I arrived at Whitworth, we decided to make a change in our benefits program. It was a no-brainer. We were adding choices to the plan. High-fives from all the employees would be their salute of appreciation. Wrong. We got a few gestures, but none of them would be on your list of ways to express appreciation. I now have a new rule: If you're going to mess with people's health care, retirement, or anything else that might affect their quality and length of life, check with them.

Most of us are involved in organizational situations in which the individual's well being is affected by the success of the whole. In some businesses, employees have so much at stake that almost all corporate decisions affect them. In gauging the degree of group member involvement needed in a decision or plan, leaders must know who the stakeholders are and the extent to which they will be affected by the outcome of the action. Democratic leadership allows the people to shape decisions and adapt to their outcomes as a part of the process. Conversely, folks who get broad-sided by top-down decrees affecting their well-being will not be very good sports when the sycophants say, "Leader knows best."

The autocratic-democratic leadership style continuum provides a very useful perspective for leaders to use in checking their operating relationships. Although some situations benefit from an authoritarian leadership style, the balance of research tips in the direction of democratic leadership being the more effective style in the 21st century. This prediction, however, is qualified by many other variables, one being the leader's attitude toward tasks and relationships.

Leading from the Middle

For the most part, democratic leaders are quite fond of the middle. But it's easy to get drawn away by other demands. The primary threat I see to the democratic leader drifting away from the middle is when the decision-making process becomes a substitute for listening to the people. This vulnerability is found more frequently in large organizations than in small, one shop enterprises. Leaders in these situations generally rely on "representatives" of the people rather than the populous itself.

For example, I am quite taken with how democratic I feel after asking the members of my cabinet to help me make an institutional decision. I can very easily get lulled into thinking I have my finger on the pulse of the organization because I got nine different perspectives on my decision. But if I'm smart, I'll walk out of that cabinet meeting and head for the Union building to chat with students, faculty and staff about issues surrounding the decision.

For any number of reasons, the members of my cabinet can give input that does not represent the perspectives of the people they represent. If I'm smart, I'll make sure I know that, regardless of the decision we end up making.

Chapter 12
Task-Oriented Leadership

One of my most memorable educational lowlights took place after a class in which my professor tested us to determine our task-relationship orientation. As a graduate student taking my first course in group dynamics, I had the blessing of studying with Em Griffin, a great human being and author of the best undergraduate communication textbook on the planet. After scoring our tests and explaining the orientation, Em asked us our scores. Well, he might as well have handed me a whip. I scored obnoxiously more task-oriented than anyone else in the class. So I tackled him after class. "Sorry, Em," I protested. "Your little test got me all wrong. I am very relationship-oriented."

Em, wanting to lighten my mood, smiled and said, "Maybe you just wish you were more relations-oriented."

"No, Em, I really am just the opposite of what this test says," I insisted.

Em chortled some lighthearted remark trying to get me to relax, but I was on a mission. I thought to myself, "Listen, Mr. Chips, you should see me in action. I'm so stinking relationship-oriented that people can't stop smiling for a week after they've been in one of my we've-got-a-lot-of-love-here groups." So I came back after him a third time, but he stopped me.

"Freeze!" he said. "Let's look at our exchange here. All I want to do is have a little relational fun with you, but you just can't let go of your task to convince me that you're not task-oriented. Think about it."

I've been thinking about it ever since.

Task-orientation in the leadership literature refers to the extent to which the leader is concerned with achieving the group's goals and getting desired results. Although task-orientation has been found in some studies to correlate with authoritarianism, theory X assumptions, and psychological distance from group members, such cold-hearted characteristics are not necessarily attributes of task-oriented leaders. These folks don't eat their young; they just want to get the job done.

My dear late mother's productivity drive bordered on the maniacal. Metaphorical to the way she lived her life was the one and only time my sister asked mom to baby-sit her infant daughter, my parents' first grandchild. When the new parents arrived home at midnight, there sat Mom, reaching across the conked-out baby in her lap, banging away furiously on her typewriter. The new parents weren't sure if the baby had fallen asleep or just passed out from the sheer exhaustion of an evening with Mom and her sacred to-do list. For people like Mom, the addiction of getting things done makes geysers out of their adrenaline glands. Granted, Mom set the task-orientation bar a bit high for the rest of humanity, and she did leave a bit of social debris in her wake, but she made mincemeat out of those to-do lists. Task-oriented leaders will confess to the rush they get from finishing their jobs.

Most studies between 1950 and 1975 found task-oriented leaders outperforming relations-oriented leaders in the area of productivity. (See Chapter 14 for situations in which relations-oriented leaders outperformed task-oriented leaders.) Even human relations champion Rensis Likert reported that a survey of several thousand workers indicated a tendency for productivity to be higher in the presence of increased pressure by supervisors for production.[1] In some groups, task-oriented leaders received higher evaluations from subordinates than relations-oriented leaders, but undoubtedly other variables influenced the assessments.

Few enterprises will prove successful without any task-oriented leaders. Frankly, I know of none. But task-orientation darkens when it becomes "task-obsession." Today's quarter-to-quarter business cycle, combined with escalating competition levels in all industries, has created enormous pressure on leaders to keep moving the needle. These conditions leave us task-driven folks swimming dangerously close to some nasty whirlpools. Regrettably, I am an expert on these waters.

Blake and Mouton argue that leaders can be both task- and relations-oriented.[2] I'll grant that possibility. In fact, when tested for these orientations, I scored moderately high on relations—to go along with my "perfect score" on task-orientation. The tyranny of the task drive, however, often whips people like me back and forth between frustration and insensitivity. When tending to relations, I'm frustrated about burning energy on something other than our goals. So then I get back in the task saddle and gallop past relational difficulties without even seeing them.

I'm sure different task-oriented people express their relational insensitivities in different ways. My way is shameful. I ignore the needs of the people closest to me. Apparently, when I'm binging on task, whatever energy I have left for relations I use on the folks "out there." I'm more likely to brush off my assistant, family, or the vice-presidents than the students or employees-at-large. In a perverse kind of way, I count on the inner circle to understand. When the task is completed, my sensitivity returns and I realize that I've been less than warm with the people I care about most.

For me, inconsistent behavior is the curse of task-orientation. I've improved at holding down my frustration and insensitivity levels by: a) redefining all tasks to include relational goals, and b) structuring interpersonal work into the task timelines. In other words, I'm not trying to abandon my task-related efforts in favor of relational work; doing so generates too much frustration. Rather, I'm reconstituting the way I think about tasks and the way I go about doing tasks to include components of relational productivity.

Leading from the Middle

Task-oriented leaders desperately need the middle. When task-oriented leaders get distracted from their groups' relational needs, leading from the middle offers a time-released antidote to their tunnel vision. In the throes of breakneck task pursuits, a very important question for task-oriented leaders to ask themselves is: "Have

I surrounded myself with the right people to get this job done in the right way?"

For example, my best fund-raising efforts find our development professionals preparing the donor in front of me; our finance and program people working on the proposal alongside of me; and our advancement staff doing follow-up work behind me. People in common pursuit of our goal have me surrounded. This configuration not only keeps me from tinkering in areas where my co-workers are more skilled than I, but it also allows me to give attention to the relational dimensions of the fund-raising.

Reflections:
Honeymoons

I've been on three honeymoons, so to speak; one with my wife and two as I've entered college presidencies. I botched the first two before having a pretty good third one. That there is a honeymoon is no fable; that the honeymoon involves a bracket of grace is no fable; but that the honeymoon offers amnesty from lasting consequences couldn't be farther from the truth. New leaders of colleges, and most other organizations, should think of their honeymoons as a couple of years in which the volume on everything they do is turned up full blast, with echoes that will be audible deep into their tenures. Unfortunately, most of us scream into the microphone. We want to show everyone it's a new day. All that junk we heard about the last president certainly won't be said of us, and we have just the right symbols to prove it.

My advice to new leaders is to think about the honeymoon as a time to be attentive and reserved, and not to be making too many style statements.

For me, learning this lesson was two parts failure and one part fluke. On our 1974 honeymoon with my wife, I wasn't attentive. On the honeymoon in my first presidency, I wasn't reserved. I probably would have blown the third honeymoon were it not for a circumstantial quirk. When I came into my current position, two factors were very different from the first time around. First, I was the fourth president (including interims) since 1986, compared to being the fourth president since 1911 in my first appointment. Second, I followed an interim president whom virtually everyone on campus hoped would become permanent (after meeting him I agreed). So I started this job somewhere between cautiously and sheepishly. Compared to my first experience, I didn't sense enormous enthusiasm for either me or for the office I was newly occupying. But I had confidence in both my experience and in bright people who loved their college and would cheer for its well-being.

I learned two lessons that are probably applicable to most organizational honeymoons. I discovered that simply being new and in-charge gave my words and actions all the amplitude they needed. When I attended a few student and faculty events I was given honeymoon credit—actually more credit than I deserved. I didn't need to be ubiquitous to be appreciated. The other happy lesson I learned was that my restraint was helping to build a reasonable foundation of expectations and hopes for the years that would follow.

Research conducted by Estela Bensimon and Robert Birnbaum, eminent researchers of college presidencies, reveals that faculty members expressing disappointment in their presidents frequently cite a loss of the president's early attentiveness and enthusiasm.[3] I guess all of this suggests that new organizational heads should repeatedly think about the question, "What kind of foundation and patterns am I developing?" As leaders, we have the obligation of a consistent tenure in both form and substance. The artificiality of our honeymoon makes it a time when we are vulnerable to excesses that can threaten the durability of our effectiveness and ultimately hollow our leadership. But I must admit, even at partial throttle, honeymoons are still fun.

Chapter 13
Relationship-Oriented Leadership

Ways of describing relations-orientation that surface in the leadership literature include "relations-centered," "concerned with people," "facilitative," "supportive," and "interactive."[1] As I noted earlier, a relations-oriented leader is one concerned with how members are feeling about their whole experience in the group. For these leaders, it is not enough simply to complete the task.

When I interviewed our director of human resources for the job she now holds, I said to her, "Your job is to help make Whitworth College a place where people love to come to work." We laugh about that rather vague job description, but we both know what it means. When people feel supported and valued, they live happier lives and do better work. I consider it both morally responsible and professionally smart for leaders to pay attention to the organization's human relations. Even the most task-oriented employee or group member longs for some measure of social support.

For the most part, experiments over the past 50 years provide evidence that job satisfaction rises in the presence of relations-oriented leadership. Specifically, a relations-orientation correlated positively with idea generation, group member self-evaluation, role clarity, communication, morale, and performance on tasks.[2] These findings come as no surprise. We all belong to groups that exist to accomplish something beyond just being a group. Intuitively, we know that when the group gets along well, more is accomplished and members are happier.

An implicit benefit found in the results of these studies is the motivational impact leaders create when they care about members' issues not directly related to the task. While working on my doctorate, I enjoyed the extraordinary tutelage of Dr. Terry Pickett who allowed me to be his friend. Much of our relationship extended beyond our tasks as student and professor. I recall writing papers that I felt had reached the "A" level, and had met my standards, but they were never done until I could picture Terry telling me what a great job I'd done. At work here was the principle of reciprocity. As my leader went beyond what was required for me, I went beyond what was required for my leader. This circularity showed me one of the most important principles of leadership I will ever learn: Leaders get what they give.

Possibly the greatest benefit that relations-oriented leaders provide their groups is putting themselves in positions to identify and remove impediments to productivity. In the early 1980s, I conducted roughly 20 market analyses in different cities around the country. My purpose was to determine area business-training needs. In each analysis I would poll managers and human-resources officers in various companies on the most salient problems in their workforces. For every technical problem reported, I'm sure I heard 50 human-relations problems. A relations-oriented leader can often see and address these difficulties before they throttle group productivity.

Freud built his psychoanalytic theory around the principle that, one way or another, we will communicate what howls within us. In the absence of a healthy outlet, the communication channel might be aberrant behavior, illness (psychosomia), or some form of inappropriate communication. The relations-oriented leader creates healthy ways to deal with the stress, ambiguity and tension that can occur naturally in a work group. The removal of these barriers enriches the members and boosts their productivity.

For three years, I reported to a very relations-oriented president. I loved just crossing paths with him in the hallway. He would whisk me into his office and pepper me with questions about my family, my job, and life in general. His generous spirit spread throughout the group who reported to him. Further, I felt his relations-orientation supported rather than supplanted, his equally strong task-orientation. There wasn't anything intrinsically wrong with his orientation, but it created dangers that all relations-oriented leaders must battle.

I'm not sure if the relational style of my charismatic boss caused me a loss of vision or a loss of nerve, but I didn't challenge him several times when, in retrospect, I should have. I didn't want to see flaws in someone who cared so deeply for me, and I for him. At the time, I wasn't even sure if they were flaws. In the long run, he and I were both hurt by my silence; and perhaps the organization suffered collateral damage as well.

Relations-oriented leaders believe rightly that their style opens lines of communication. However, they have to work very intentionally to tease out the concerns of their people. I know I could have spoken up, but usually I didn't, and I never wanted to. He didn't need it, I thought. Exacerbating the problem, he wore his job pressures on his sleeve. So his countenance said "Talk to me," while the arm encased by the "job pressure" sleeve pushed away anything that might add to his load.

The ability to send this particular mixed message rubbed off on me. Even when I'm feeling particularly relations-oriented I should put a sign on my door that says, "Ignore my efforts to look busy and come right in, because I really do care about what you have to say."

Groups led by relations-oriented leaders can have a difficult time identifying and reporting problems, especially those caused in some way by the leaders. The groups must be provided with opportunities that invite expressions of concern.

Another danger faced by relations-oriented leaders poses a special threat in groups or organizations where the leader does not have direct contact with all group members. In Section I, I made the argument that most 21st century organizations will be geographically dispersed. By virtue of proximity, some people enjoy more time with the leader than others. It comes naturally to relational leaders to form close relationships with the people they encounter frequently. In the eyes of some, this creates a relational unevenness that smacks of favoritism.

Perhaps some leaders possess the emotional discipline to prevent frequency of contact from deepening a relationship, but that doesn't change people's perceptions of the "inner circle," and holding the high-contact people at bay runs against the grain of relations-oriented leaders. More than with some dangers, this is one where being forewarned is being forearmed. Taking every opportunity to connect beyond the natural contact group helps even the balance of relationships. Because I do have friends and sports cronies with whom I work, I'm especially sensitive to the "favorites" criticism. So I spend more time than many supervisors doing "relational wandering around." And, actually, that also helps me better understand my task.

Leading from the Middle

Relations-oriented leaders often get caught in cross currents. Meeting the challenges of their tasks pulls them in one direction while their affinity for doing social maintenance carries them in another. These people need the middle in order to work from their strengths. Even for relational leaders, the task current is strong and can sweep them away from contact with behind-the-scenes group members. Dwelling among the people puts these leaders in a position to satisfy their relational inclinations with the whole group. You can't tend to the group members' feelings and relations of group members by remote control. I've tried it, and I've failed. When relations-oriented leaders lose touch with the people, they lose valuable "I care" chips and efforts to reconnect ring hollow. Questions of sincerity rise.

It's all right for leadership scholars to identify a relations-orientation as a "style," but caring for others as simply a "style" doesn't sell with the rank and file. For them, leaders must demonstrate the substance of authentic concern in attending to group-member relations. Intermittent grins and backslaps don't cut it. The middle of the group guides, fine tunes, and even corrects the leaders whose care they have learned to appreciate.

REFLECTIONS:
THE CREDIT BOOMERANG

The first few years after my father retired from a 29-year stint overseeing a program he founded, it seemed to me he was neglected by those who carried on his work. He probably wasn't, and the sudden removal of attention didn't seem to faze him. After all, this was the man who had so little ego that when, at the Moody Bible Institute's Founder's Week, the 1974 Moody alumnus of the year was being described, he whispered to my mother, "It's amazing how much this guy has in common with me."

To which she incredulously replied, "Paul, it is you."

I'll never forget Dad's confused expression as I looked over my mother's shoulder and realized that he was the only one of the 2,500 people present who was still in suspense.

When I entered the presidency, I followed a man who, like my father, had done his job well for 30 years; and remembering my father, I took every opportunity to tell the world what a fine job my predecessor had done. I vowed to myself that even at the risk of people bemoaning his departure, I would honor his leadership. What I discovered was the impossibility of diminishing perceptions of my effectiveness by exalting his. Credit is not a finite entity that is exhaustible when distributed. It gains energy and magnitude when freely given. Leaders need to keep themselves in a salutary frame of mind.

I have learned this credit lesson well, but I still fail, more often than not, to practice it. My ego-less father taught us repeatedly that we could accomplish much if we didn't care about receiving credit, and he was right. But I'm afraid I have taken the lesson a step too far—acting as though credit shouldn't matter to anyone. At times I find myself agreeing with Pericles, who was reluctant to eulogize fallen warriors, believing their accomplishments should not be judged on the basis of how well he praised them. The big difference between Pericles and me is that the people I work with aren't dead and need to feel appreciated, whether I think it's important or not. In this respect, the Golden Rule sometimes lets people like me down and should be rewritten to read, "Do unto others as they would have you do unto them."

I suspect that when I fail to notice the need to give praise, it is my "ideal" self rather than my "real" self that is shrugging off the importance of credit. In my next ten years, there will be more "thank you's" and more gold stars as I keep clearly in mind the self-perpetuating nature of credit.

Chapter 14

Leadership Style Interactions

It is very difficult to examine styles in a vacuum. "It all depends" keeps qualifying our claims and conclusions. Studies that attempt to shed light on how the effectiveness of a leader's style depend on the situation come up short in fully explaining and predicting leadership effectiveness. Other interaction effects influence leadership style before the leader even gets to the situation. We have identified "authoritarian or democratic" and "task/result-orientation or relations-orientation" as the two most enduring style dimensions.

Before looking at how situations affect the success of these two style continuums, it is helpful to consider briefly how they interact with each other.

Basic Leadership Style Interactions

For the most part, authoritarian leaders tend to dwell in the task/results-driven side while democratic leaders usually lean toward a relations-orientation. Occasionally, these orientations cross. For example, I combine a strong task-orientation with a democratic style of decision-making. As such, I am vulnerable to excesses from which the other three combinations are pretty safe. Below I combine the two orientations and suggest the principal threats to the effectiveness of each combination. We need to be aware what twists we bring with our styles in dealing with different situations.

	Task-oriented	Relations-oriented
Authoritarian	Authoritarian Task-oriented (A-T)	Authoritarian Relations-oriented (A-R)
Democratic	Democratic Task-oriented (D-T)	Democratic Relations-oriented (D-R)

I offer two suggestions if you wish to place yourself in the appropriate quadrant: first, test your self-perception against how others perceive you to make sure your classification isn't what you want, rather than how you usually function; second, realize that this is a very general orientation that won't hold in all situations.

Authoritarian-Task-Oriented

Shame on me for mentioning Mike Ditka in connection with leadership, but he serves well as an example of this style going over the top. I lived in Chicago when Ditka took the Bears to the Superbowl. He regularly criticized his coaches and players as he cracked the whip en route to a National Football League championship. To say the least, he got the job done. Amid Chicago's excitement over "da Bears," a sportswriter observed that Ditka's harsh style accumulated enemies along the way, and when the Bears started to lose, Ditka would get dumped. That commentary forecast turned out to be prophetic, as the coach failed to survive even one losing season.

Regardless of what motivates this A-T style, I find it treacherously high-risk. Acceptance by the group lasts only as long as the group's success. In other words, leaders with this style have no room for failure when it comes to group support. What looks strong and purposeful in the context of success comes across as arbitrary and obsessive when things go bad.

A-T leaders should do everything possible to communicate the rationale behind their decisions while reminding the group of the mutual benefits of success. Further, neither an autocratic style nor a task-orientation forces the A-T leader to abandon warmth and kindness. Such leaders have no excuse to not be cordial.

I worked with Bob Keck, a member of a well-known international law firm. Keck was utterly task-oriented, very authoritarian, but always caring and congenial. Unfortunately, autocratic task-oriented leaders do not always follow Keck's example and place "kind" as a high priority.

Authoritarian-Relations-Oriented

Watch out for "The Parent" smiling at you from the A-R style. For several years, a person who spent the early part of his career in the military ran an operation that reported to me. Coursing through this man's blood was a majestic sense of hierarchy. Proper channels and chain of command formed the passages through which he maneuvered his life. The man was also very relationship-oriented, caring deeply for the feelings and well-being of his department. Not surprisingly, people often responded to him as a dad. Both adoration and rebellion surfaced in the various reactions to his leadership. His warm, authoritarian grip felt condescending to some and secure to others.

After watching this style closely, my advice to A-R leaders is threefold:

1. Always avoid paternalistic tones in communication.

2. Ask your people too many, rather than too few, questions about the strategies and goals of your tasks—they need to see themselves as your advisers, not as your children.

3. Stick a small "Do not enter" sign by your office door, and look at it every time your relations-orientation tempts you to let conversations leave office matters and enter personal ones. Otherwise, you are vulnerable to becoming a "parent-confessor" for your people.

Democratic-Task-Oriented

Here I write from experience. Actually, I'm certain the folks who report to me could write volumes on the excesses of this combination. First of all, D.T. leaders can whine like there's no tomorrow. Generally, they drive with "the pedal to the metal" while the emergency brake is crammed all the way to the floor. This metaphor was not a metaphor when recently I was screaming dramatically to the car gods for an answer to what was "wrong with my stinking car," (popping that emergency brake really makes a thud after driving until it melts to the floorboard).

Frustration is as much a part of life as breathing for task-oriented leaders who stay in a hurry to get things done mode but realize that the group can almost always outperform their individual efforts in the quality of task accomplishment. They choose the quality of democracy over the efficiency of autocracy, and it drives them crazy.

Related to the frustration felt by the D.T. leader is an attendant sense of impatience communicated to the group. I catch myself conjuring up more urgency than most situations merit. I think I'm aware of the time it takes to do things well, so I want everybody to get cracking. If I'm not careful, my non-verbal communication makes a mockery of my verbal attempts at social maintenance before we get down to business.

Finally, task-oriented leaders who believe in the democratic process often delegate in ways that fail to provide adequate direction to the delegates. When we believe in our people and are driven to be productive, delegation is the answer. The problems arise when the leader's focus on his or her tasks prevents following up on the tasks that have been delegated to others. It is essential for democratic-task-oriented leaders to structure follow-up and feedback into their work relationships. In my opinion, this combination, more than any other, requires regular individual and group meetings.

Democratic-Relations-Oriented

Leaders favoring this style present themselves as "first among equals," but they're not first by much. They place importance on everyone being involved (democratic) and getting along (relations-oriented). As a general leadership orientation this combination threatens a group's focus and productivity. In a horserace, this style would finish dead last, but the jockey, owner, trainer, and investors would all make room for each other on the back of the poor mare, and there would be lots of love up there.

I was introduced to the excess of this style when I sat down with a friend to discuss several of my concerns about a director. He summed up my impression by observing, "He's become more of a mascot than a manager." I am convinced that groups whose leaders have generally democratic styles (both task-oriented and relations-oriented) want the person at the top to be more decisive.

For me, my task-orientation comes to the rescue when the democratic process bogs down. I have observed, however, that when the democratic process gets sluggish for highly relations-oriented leaders, their instincts betray them. Sensing frustration among group members, they attempt to draw direction and resolution from the group, wrongly assuming that more of the same relational emphasis will keep everyone happy. Under these conditions, you can bet some group member would like to throw a striped shirt and a whistle at the leader and yell, "Make the call."

I offer two questions to D.R. leaders that I use every time the voice of my task-orientation tells me that the democratic process has become "analysis paralysis." First: Is there more information forthcoming that will improve the quality of the action? Second: Are we missing anybody that could improve our decision? If the answer comes up "no" to these questions, we move. Every day, democratic-relations-oriented leaders should pledge allegiance to the completion of their tasks. Their group members will be glad that they did.

Chapter 15
Situational Leadership

Several months ago I had an interesting "leadership" day. At
7:45 a.m. I met with the whole staff of the college. Six times
a year we meet for 30 minutes to get caught up with each
other. At noon I had a meeting with twelve corporate CEOs and
the presidents of five universities on a committee that I co-chair.
At 3 p.m. I met with the "president's cabinet," consisting of the
people who report to me.

In the first group, my position as president held significance in
my efforts to inspire and inform the people. In the second group,
my position held no immediate relevance to my role as convener
and facilitator. On one side of me sat the president of a large land-
grant research university, and next to him sat the majority owner of
a publicly traded hotel chain. Neither of those two guys moved to
the edge of their seats when the Whitworth president spoke. In the
third meeting with my cabinet, being president held intermittent
significance. I served roles as supervisor, group member, listener,
informer, and occasionally president, as we discussed the operations of the college.

Situation theorists believe that these three different meetings
called for three different leadership styles. What they call "situational moderators" influence the effectiveness of different
approaches. For example, if we look only at my task and relations-
orientation in these meetings, the different leadership needs
become clear. In the first meeting, I need to lead from a warm, relationship-oriented base. The task of communicating information
ranks behind how we feel about one another. In the second meet-

ing, both relations and task emphases are needed. I possess no "authority" as leader in this volunteer group, so a strong relations-orientation is required to make folks feel good about their participation. But it is never long before I feel the need to get very task-oriented in order to get things done. The conviviality of the group belies their demand that we achieve. The third group needs my task-orientation after a short time of social and spiritual renewal. We meet weekly, we like each other, and we don't like wasting time, but we're all smart-alecs and we have a tendency to horse around during everyone's agenda items except our own. So I need to be intermittently task-oriented without messing up the group chemistry we all enjoy.

Style Adaptability

Before reviewing the most significant ways that style and situation relate to each other, I want to comment on four ways of thinking about the "adaptability" of a person's leadership style. All four philosophies have been suggested, both implicitly and explicitly, by various leadership authors over the past 50 years.

Get the right leader for the situation. This "different horses for different courses" approach rests on the assumption that leaders possess a dominant style. Matching these preferred styles with the situations that call for them results in a good leadership environment.

Teach the leader to adapt to the situation. Theorists holding this position believe situations shift too frequently to keep changing leaders, as set forth in the first approach. Leaders should learn to adjust their styles and emphases. Shifting lines every two minutes works better in playing hockey than in leading groups.

Strong leaders change the situation to suit their strengths. My elementary-school gym teacher was a Marine. We did nothing but march in three of our five weekly classes. I didn't stop liking it until fifth grade when I found out we were the only school in America with pre-pubescent battalions snapping to attention after 55 minutes of synchronized walking. To the four-year-old with a hammer, the world becomes a nail. In like manner, some leaders with a dominant, well-honed style see every situation as one that needs just what they have to offer.

Situations create leadership styles. This philosophy combines the first two and is held more often by historians than by leadership theorists. Proponents of this approach would defend the styles of Gerald Ford and Jimmy Carter as products of the post-Nixon era. The national political climate created by Nixon shaped the leadership styles of Ford and Carter.

In Section I, I discussed the need for "paradoxical leadership," a style that demands adaptability. As a behavioral scientist, I believe internal and external forces sculpt a leadership pre-disposition in all of us. Transformational leadership, which has captured the interests of late 20th-Century theorists (see Chapter 16), places its faith in the ability of leaders to be adaptive. In presenting the contingency models of situational leadership, I assume—or hope—that leaders can change. If nothing else, an awareness of situational differences should lift their sensitivity to factors beyond their own inclinations.

Fiedler's Contingency Model

No leadership model has generated more research than Fred Fiedler's contingency model.[1] As one of the first theorists to examine the relationship between style and situation, Fiedler ignited an interest that dominated the field for almost 25 years. I find it very interesting that in spite of Fiedler's profound influence, he is one of the only leadership theorists of his era to believe that leadership styles are somewhat intractable. His first choice for creating effective leadership would be to find the leader with the style needed for the situation. If that couldn't happen, Fiedler would advise the leader to try changing the situation. He believed that leaders could change situations more easily than they could change their own spots.

The contingency model of leadership looks at style in terms of task versus relationship orientation. I use "versus" advisedly. Fiedler didn't think the leader could be high in both. I, and many of his colleagues, disagree; however, I haven't seen too many leaders in whom one of these two orientations doesn't predominate. "Situation," in this model, referred to the favorability of the conditions. Fiedler defined very favorable conditions as ones in which a) the leader and group members had a good relationship, b) the task was clear, and c) the leader had positional authority. The most unfavorable conditions existed when none of those elements were present.[2]

I first studied Fiedler's findings in 1975. In virtually every leadership situation since, I have found myself "checking with Fred" to size up what is needed. Fiedler discovered:

- In extremely favorable conditions, a task-oriented leader proves more effective in accomplishing the work.
- In moderate conditions, the relations-oriented leader does better.
- In very unfavorable conditions, the task-oriented leader will be the more effective leader.

Fiedler breaks down the conditions very specifically and reports different findings for different combinations of the three situation components. My use of his work has been more basic. I ask myself five questions to size up the situation in groups I am assigned to lead:

1. What is the reason for this group's existence? Answering this question helps me to answer the second question.

2. What expectations does the group have of my role? I need to consider what the group wants from my leadership.

3. What is our task? I wrap goal, objective, strategy and tactic differentiations into a general measure of task clarity. By establishing a sense of "task-readiness," I can avoid wasting energy on ambiguous task dead-ends.

4. What is the condition of the group? Again, I'm trying to determine a readiness factor. Either too little or too much time spent on relations can impede group progress. On this point I would add (audaciously, I admit) one factor to Fiedler's "situation favorability" conditions. Earlier, I made the distinction between "instrumental" and "consummatory" reasons for joining a group. Some folks join only for what the group produces, while others might participate largely for the affiliation. I find it helpful to assess whether some members have joined the group largely for affiliation purposes. For them, the task is the group. Those of us who greet the group, jump on the bulldozer, plow our way to the end of the task, and then leave instantly are not the perfect leaders for these folks.

5. Is this group a rocket waiting to be launched or a sack of parts waiting to be assembled? In other words, is this a really good or a really bad situation? I know that my task-orientation lends itself to very good and very bad situations. Under such conditions, I don't need to spend too much time talking to myself. I can engage in a little social gesturing, drop a load of hurry on the group, and we're off. Under moderate conditions, I find it helpful to think of myself in the dual role of human-relations coordinator and task champion.

The thought rather haunts me that our styles might be as impermeable as Fiedler believed. In fact, Section III of this book rests on the assumption that we can change. But before moving on to a model based on the adaptability of our styles, I offer one tip that I wish I would always remember: Lean into the wind. As you embark on leadership roles, if you are predisposed toward task, think group relations. If your natural inclination is to focus on relations, think task.[3]

Three Situational Variables

I feel the interaction between a person's leadership orientation and the favorability of the situation represents the most basic variable affecting leadership effectiveness. We hold greater access to our own behaviors and attitudes than to those of the group. Further, shuffling leaders around to fit situations works well in experimental settings, but in real life we often need to work with the hands we're dealt. Sensitive leaders who know what to look for can adapt to most of the situational curves thrown at them.

Sensitivity to the presence and influence of three situational factors will serve leaders well to the extent that the leaders adapt their dominant styles.

1. Perceived power of the leader. I do not believe that "leader position power"[4] or "the authority given by the organization" is as important as the power that followers give to their leader. Young Life, Inc., an interdenominational ministry to junior high and high school students, pounds the mandate into every one of its staff members that "You have to win the kids every day." In that same respect, I believe leadership power is "won" more than assigned. Few would argue that as long as group members have a choice, only they can grant a leader the power to influence. But do leaders really operate on the assumption that their followers are their most important source of power?

A leader approaches every situation with different kinds of power.[5] The nature and degree of power in groups has captivated the attention of several consultants and behavioral scientists. French and Raven's power bases include:

• *Expert power:* group members' perception of the leader's competence

• *Referent power:* group members' identification with or general fondness of the leader

• *Reward power:* group members' perception of the leader's ability to provide rewards

• *Coercive power:* group members' perception of the leader's ability to evoke punishment

• *Legitimate power:* group members' belief that the leader has "the right" to lead (includes "positional power")

I have been offered three other types of power in various forms:

• *Information power:* group members' perception that the leader has valuable information

• *Goodwill power:* group members' perception that the leader cares about their well-being

• *Short-straw power:* group members' assignment of leader status without a substantive basis (other than that they need someone in the role).

The fundamental question leaders should ask themselves in assessing the conditions of every leadership situation is, "Why me? What do the group members feel I bring to this situation that will prompt them to accept my leadership?" The answer to this question inevitably draws upon several power bases. If we fail to ask the question, or to answer it correctly, the following four problems may result:

Assuming the wrong base. On occasion, academic deans will discover academic department chairs assuming levels of expert power and legitimate power when other members of the department are granting little more than short-straw power. These chairs must earn perceptions of expertise and legitimacy if they hope to function in any role beyond coordinator.

Squandering a base. The first capital campaign consultant I retained after I became a college president drove me crazy. Supposedly, this person's reservoir of experience formed a strong base of expertise. Yet her mode of operation was to finesse out of us what we wanted to do, and then slap our hand if we failed to meet the timeline. We granted this person a truckload of expert power, but getting substantive advice out of her bordered on the impossible. She did little more than keep us on schedule.

Depleting a base. This problem occurs when we fail to recognize that our power almost always emerges from an arrangement of bases, rather than from one exclusively. For example, giving orders without explanation can allow our bases of expertise and information power to atrophy while exhausting our referent or legitimate power. Parents exploit their coercion power when they bark to their children, "Because I say so!" C'mon, Dad, tap into a few other bases. Nobody wants on their epitaph, "His strong suit was coercion."

Ignoring a base. A significant vulnerability tags along with my conviction that, essentially, my leadership power is granted to me by those I lead. I err in the under-use of my legitimate power. Sometimes group members have to bleed it out of me. I explain, I inform, I charm, and I talk about the abundant rewards as I dance around various bases, inviting my cabinet to grant me power. I know I have ignored my legitimate base when, in the middle of one of these performances, someone says, "Bill, make a decision." Sometimes we fail to notice the power bases that can strengthen our leadership.

Perceptions people hold of their leaders' power exert huge influence over the leadership situation. Leaders must direct and moderate their styles depending on the nature and degree of their power. Too often we overlook the "Why me?" question.

2. Trend-line of the group or organization. Hardly anything causes me to adjust my leadership style as much as the general health and success rate of the group I'm leading. I find this situational variable exercising a profound influence on my leadership instincts. Because of my job, I think of conditions affecting the whole organization.

I'm not sure that I ever consciously choose to alter my style on the basis of prosperity and morale, but I know that I do. As president of a college, I find myself attempting to supply what I fear the organization could lose. Hence, I find myself leading with a style that runs counter to the trend-line—the prevailing direction of organizational strength and employee morale. In the challenging times, I'm pretty upbeat. When prosperity returns, I have a tendency to work with a furrowed brow.

I have assumed the presidencies of two colleges in the midst of declining enrollments. In considering whether to accept the jobs at both institutions, I didn't really think the task of increasing enrollments would be all that formidable at either place. Both places had good missions and strong histories. There were plenty of areas that scared me, but I felt pretty sure I knew which buttons to push for attracting and retaining students. My confidence, coupled with the prevailing fears of the faculty and staff, prompted me to exude optimism. I served not only as president, but also as cheerleader and soothsayer. I wanted folks to know that our great mission and great people were a "can't miss" combination.

As enrollment fortunes reversed in both situations, so did my style. I became more task-oriented and less rah-rah. I worked harder. We had all hustled like mad to turn things around, and I didn't want a sense of complacency to undermine our progress. Inspiring hope when things looked discouraging and providing urgency when the future looked rosy represented efforts to supply what I didn't want the colleges to lose.

I learned about the importance of urgency in reacting to a trend-line at Princeton Theological Seminary. My best friend there, Ken West, was a great tennis player who now writes wonderful books on parenting and human development. Ken would spot me 13 points in a squash match, and then play me to 15. When I got good, he granted me only 12 points. During various sports, I noticed that when Ken got on some kind of a scoring streak (which was often), his already high intensity level would just shoot off the chart. It didn't even look like he was having fun. When I asked him what demon invaded his body when he got on a roll, he gave me an answer I've never forgotten. In essence he told me that the fiercest enemy of momentum is momentum. When you're on a roll, everything feels easy; none of the voices within you push you to work harder. In other words, momentum breeds a complacency you must battle with all of your energy. Momentum is what we work to achieve, and it requires almost more work to keep it than to get it.

Leaders must watch the progress of the groups they lead, and then supply the kind of leadership that is needed. As they move their groups through the inevitable rises and dips, it's important for leaders to think about how their styles can be used to offset the attitudinal imbalances created by prosperity swings. Many times leaders will find that a bit of a style change invigorates their organizations.

At a conference of college presidents, a group of us discussed the vanishing breed of long-tenured presidents. We concluded that it is still possible for one person, but not one "presidency," to serve effectively over the long haul. In other words, a leader must make fundamental adjustments in style and emphasis for the group (the college, in this case) to stay relevant and fresh. As conditions change, the leader must adapt. Both the organization and the leader will benefit.

3. Psychological needs of group members My observations about trend-lines apply primarily to entire organizations. In considering psychological needs, I'm referring to individuals and small groups—particularly to the leaders' immediate working groups. On a grand scale, I provide leadership for Whitworth College, but to get that done, I give direct leadership to the ten people who report to me. It is this group whose psychological needs I must consider in calculating adaptations I need to make to my leadership style.

Any discussion of the interaction between leadership style and psychological frameworks must include Paul Hersey and Ken Blanchard's Situational Leadership Model. Their model attempts to match the best leadership behavior with the maturity level of the group members. Their hypotheses are more applicable to the superior-subordinate relationship in an organization than to volunteer-based groups.

A good bit of controversy swirls around the Situational Leadership Model. Bass observes, "the Hersey-Blanchard model has had remarkably widespread intuitive appeal to practicing managers and to leaders of management training programs, despite its theoretical inadequacies and the paucity of supportive empirical evidence."[6] Criticisms notwithstanding, situational leadership has become one of the most enduring management tools of the 20th century. The essence of the theory can be briefly summarized:

• Managers are most effective when they are able to diagnose their subordinates' "willingness" (attitude or confidence) and their ability to perform the task before them. There are four readiness levels of followers and four associated management styles based on these readiness levels.

Readiness Level 1: low ability and low willingness. Leadership style: telling (highly structured task arrangement and low consideration of relationships). Metaphor: drill sergeant with draftees. The leader has to provide direction while exercising some kind of power to create productivity.

Readiness Level 2: low ability and high willingness. Leadership style: coaching or selling. Metaphor: Football coach with an eager young quarterback, itching to get in the game. The leader's job is to continue to teach the skills (high task) while offering high levels of consideration, helping the subordinates feel good about who they are and about their progress.

Readiness Level 3: high ability and low willingness. Leadership style: participation or encouragement. Metaphor: supervisor of gifted salesperson who would rather do almost anything than make the calls. Leader's job is to instill confidence by enthusiastically reinforcing success and encouraging effort.

Readiness Level 4: high ability and high willingness. Leadership style: delegation. Metaphor: The admiring violin teacher who works with a pupil on musicality and repertoire, never having to bark, "Practice!" The leader works with this subordinate by delegating the right tasks, then getting out of the way and cheering successes.

• In general, psychologically immature groups and group members benefit most from a strong task-orientation. Mature groups and group members benefit most from a strong relations-orientation.

• The most effective leaders possess both high task- and relations-orientations and adjust their style to the maturity levels of those being led.[7]

In my view, the greatest benefit provided by this model is in prompting the leader to look beyond task and relational issues to the psychological needs of the group.

I believe that the best way for us to adapt our styles to a person's psychological needs is to take a run through my altered version of the Golden Rule: Do unto others as they would like you to do unto them. This rule provides an antidote for judging other people's needs on the basis of our own (closer to the real Golden Rule, but not as effective).

When I was an academic dean, an assistant dean reported to me. I had not chosen him; he was a gift, as it were, from my provost. I thought this colleague was toting a generously sized ego when he pouted to me about how devastated he felt over my failure to introduce him properly to a group of faculty members. I didn't overhaul the style with which I dealt with him until the day he bounded into my office and asked if he could trade his new salary increase for the more gallant title of "associate" dean. "Sure," I bubbled, and a happier, albeit poorer, associate dean left my office. We got along better when I understood his values and needs.

We can make very helpful style adjustments to provide psychological support to the folks for whom we provide leadership. It requires attentiveness to notice their needs, compassion to provide for those needs, and humility to keep ourselves from thinking they should have different needs—ours, for example. Without being duplicitous or loosening their integrity, good leaders treat different people differently. That's part of the art of leadership, but we must also know our own psychological limits. I'm wretched with tender egos. I'm not as bad as I was when I shamelessly let that associate dean give back his raise, but I'm still not very good.

To adjust our styles to other folks' needs, we need to understand our own. For some people we don't have an adjustment in our kit that will work. We can't lead them and we shouldn't try. A change in groups by at least one of us offers the best bet for both to be happy. But for everyone else, our ability to lead will rest on sensitivity to their needs and our capacity to adjust our style appropriately.

Former U.S. Senator from Oregon Mark Hatfield once said that his biggest challenge as an elected official was discerning when to lead those who put him in office and when to represent those who put him in office. Most members of Congress will find that one approach comes more naturally than the other. In some respects, the leader of a group or organization looks at similar choices and has corresponding pre-dispositions. When should leading be leader-centered and when should it be group-centered?

Leadership studies suggest that leaders carry natural inclinations toward authoritarian or democratic leadership into their organizations. Evidence also supports the claim that organizational situations shape the styles of their leaders. It is safe to say that the majority of the studies concluded that, in general, a democratic leadership style outperformed an authoritarian style in the areas of group-member satisfaction and productivity (as measured in the long run). But exceptions to this general finding abounded, as some groups, depending on the situation, experienced better results under authoritarian leadership.

During the middle of the 20th-century, most theorists believed that leaders' tendencies surfaced in styles that matched better with some organizational situations than others. As we consider recent trends in leadership theory, matching leaders' styles with the right situations will give way to the philosophy that good leaders bend their leadership orientations in order to adapt to the changing needs of an organization. That trend will absolutely blast its way into the 21st century.

Leading from the Middle

I am plagued, and occasionally blessed, by many off-campus involvements. Most of them hold strategic potential for advancing the college, but valuable or not, they take me away. When I am not traveling, family and civic duties crowd my schedule. I serve on a lot of boards, chairing a couple of them, including the Spokane Region Chamber of Commerce. And, more importantly, I serve as a husband and as a father to my children, one of whom is still at home and deserves my undivided attention.

All of these duties compete with my efforts to lead from the middle. Much of the time I'm not anywhere near the borders of our college. I have realized that all of these external duties make barging my way into the middle of our people more important than ever. It has become very clear to me that the less time I spend in the midst of the people and programs of Whitworth College, the more programmed my leadership style becomes. Conversely, I find myself far more adaptive when I'm moving among our people. I don't know if distance causes me to lose my sensitivity or my confidence, or both. Maybe the piles of accumulated work that greet my return force me into a rigid get-it-done style. Whatever the reasons, I know that the middle makes me more nimble and adaptable.

Several weeks ago, I met with three people who wield a lot of influence over my schedule. Going into that meeting, it was important for me to have a clear sense of which college events brought me into the nexus of college community life. This past year I fell well below my average on time spent in the middle. Receding campus involvement triggered my leadership default settings, and my style became stiffly task-oriented. If I hope to avoid a repeat of last year, I must know the most efficient paths to the middle, then elbow my way past the opportunities that attempt to pull me off the paths. This is largely why the first semester of next year I have chosen to tether myself to campus. From experience, I know how the middle can elevate our capacity to make needed adjustments in the way we lead.

Section IV
Transformational Leadership

T he final era of the 20th Century is one in which the potential to exercise leadership reached every member in every corner of the organization. The authoritarian leaders of centralized organizations in 1900 would not recognize the decentralized distribution of leadership that represents the 21st century ideal. At the dawn of the 20th century, who would have pictured the most venerated leadership expert in America suggesting that leaders establish a relationship of mutual stimulation and elevation that converts followers into leaders and may convert leaders into moral agents?[1]

The other night my wife and I watched Jack Lemmon in the old movie, *The Apartment*. From that wonderful flick, I would conclude that even 40 years ago it would have been a chore to find very many followers who had been converted into leaders.

I have divided the two chapters on transformational leadership into what it looks like from the leader's perspective and how it can be instilled in those members of the group who "report to the leader." My treatment of this era very briefly summarizes the concepts and characteristics of transformational leadership. It is also over laden with my own perspective.[2]

Chapter 16
Transformational Leadership

A soccer coach, nicknamed Thor, used to coach for our school. To label Thor as stoic would be like characterizing the Pacific Ocean as wet. Thor's bench style was inert. When the match reached a fever pitch, we would watch Thor for any signs of what physicians call "a pulse." When Thor lowered his brow, we would all speculate what might be causing his temper tantrum. To say the least, Thor was understated. But, oh, how his boys could play soccer. "Spirited" is a mild euphemism for their furious intensity. And they seldom lost.

The trait theorists would have had to spend an entire season in Thor's back pocket to find the personal attributes that made him a great coach. But looking at Thor through the prism of transformational leadership yields immediate and significant findings. By the time matches began, Thor had skillfully transferred his leadership to the men on the field. Followers had been transformed into leaders, working toward a common goal worthy of demoting any individual objectives. Thor exerted what we call a transforming influence over his team, in spite of his frozen demeanor.

It's easier to point to Thor's influence than to come up with the definition of transformational leadership. Actually, there is no one, agreed-upon, definition. We shouldn't be surprised; if scholars can't agree on a definition for leadership, the odds are slim that adding the rather slippery adjective, transformational, will clear things up. Fortunately, the term carries enough properties common to all definitions for us to understand what it means. In my opinion it is well worth the effort to peel back the layers and look at this very holistic way to think about leadership.

Starting with the ideas of several experts in transformational leadership will help us surround, if not define, the term.

James MacGregor Burns. Not to confuse a Scot with a Spaniard, but Burns is the Picasso of leadership thought. His 1978 work represented a different way to think about the art of leadership, and virtually all leadership studies since have been influenced by his work. Burns says that transforming leadership is a "relationship of mutual stimulation and elevation that converts followers into leaders and may convert leaders into moral agents."[1] He continues, saying that transforming leadership is "evolving interrelationships in which leaders are continuously evoking motivational responses from followers and modifying their behavior as they meet responsiveness or resistance, in a ceaseless process of flow and counterflow."[2]

Departing from the emphases on leader-centered traits and behaviors, Burns's notion of leadership focuses on mutuality, process and adaptation. Burns also campaigned harder for the moral dimensions of leadership than most theorists who went before him.

Bernard Bass. Yukl summarizes well Bass's notion of transformational leadership. "The extent to which a leader is transformational is measured primarily in terms of the leader's effect on followers. Followers of a transformational leader feel trust, admiration, loyalty and respect toward the leader, and they are motivated to do more than they originally expected to do. These leaders elevate the importance of the task, inspire followers to put the group interests before their own, and 'activate their higher-order needs'."[3]

Bass (1985) built on the work of Burns (1978), and many theorists believe that the outcomes of Burns's transforming leadership parallel those of Bass's transformational leadership, even though the definitions differ. The big difference between Burns and Bass lies in the nature of motivation. Where Burns heralded morality as essential to transforming leadership, Bass inserted nobility.

Gary Yukl. I like Yukl's clarity in almost everything he writes. He defines transformational leadership simply as, "the process of building commitment to the organization's objectives and empowering followers to accomplish these objectives."

The succinctness of this definition leaves it a bit closer to "pre-transformational" theories than the way Yukl unpacks it in his book. But Yukl's cornerstones of "process," "commitment," and "empowerment" still support the foundation of transformational leadership. Style and situational theorists would consider these elements superfluous to the leadership needed in some situations.

Characteristics of Transformational Leadership

Based on my studies, experiences and efforts, I have come to believe that transformational leadership relies on three characteristics: authentic, adaptive, and interactive. I am not suggesting that these three elements are all one needs to be a transformational leader. In fact, I am assuming the pre-existence of a basic leadership capacity. But I have come to believe that the presence of these dimensions is what differentiates transforming leadership from the trait-based or style-based models. In order to meet the requirements of Burns's lofty definition, transforming leadership must be authentic, adaptive and interactive. Remove any one of the three, and Burns's description crumbles.

Authentic: Roughly 10 years ago, I found myself seated in front of the presidential search committee at a prestigious non-sectarian university. This meeting concluded three days of preening around campus as one of two finalists for the job of running the school. Amid all the fanfare, both my wife and I felt disquieted over the way in which several faculty members brandished their "open-mindedness" as they raised concerns that I might be influenced by my faith. Evidently, their liberalism wasn't liberal enough to make room for faith. So I was feeling a bit confused and agitated when the search committee concluded our three days by asking me if I'd seen anything I didn't like about their university.

This question triggered what became my leadership moment of truth. I replied, "Yes. Your mission statement is built around the claim that you 'search for excellence, wherever it may be found.' I'm not sure what that means. Frankly, I haven't been able to figure out the soul of this university."

Without knowing it at the time, I was really talking to myself as much as to them. That experience awakened me to a bright awareness that my image of being a leader placed an authentic commitment to mission squarely in the middle of the picture. In other words, my understanding of a leader was of a "transforming" leader.

You can't fake transformational leadership. I do not believe leaders can boost followers to transcendent levels just by going through the right motions. I think transformational leaders must be absolutely sold on the mission of their organizations. I admit that in one respect, transformational leadership reaches back to the situational models. Leaders must be selective in choosing to lead only in groups and situations where they can provide authentic enthusiasm for the mission. It's at this point that I accept the distinction between managing operations and leading change. A good manager can be effective in far more situations than a transformational leader can. Good management requires delivering the right style for the operational demands of the situation. I don't think transformation occurs unless a leader brings to the organization or group a deep belief in the fundamental importance of the mission. Without that conviction, efforts to bring group members to higher moral planes, or to inspire them to put the group needs in front of their individual needs, will ring hollow.

When I received a call about Whitworth, it was from the same headhunter who'd led the presidential search in which I couldn't seem to find the soul of the institution. He claimed to have the perfect school for me. On paper, Whitworth had two strikes against it. First, the institution was in a bit of a bad mood. Several years of struggle over enrollments and finances had stirred the faculty and undoubtedly contributed to the prior president's decision to leave suddenly. I had enjoyed enough success in my short career to allow me to select my way around that kind of a deal. Second, Whitworth presented itself as a Christian college. I have great respect for most Christian colleges, but I wasn't sure how well I would fit in one. Though firmly committed to the Christian faith, I did not believe that a colleges could huddle behind walls of orthodoxy and achieve academic superiority.

At many Christian colleges, hard questions posed as threats rather than as sharpening stones. As a Christian I stood, and still stand, with Martin Luther in believing God is a mighty fortress who dwelt among us as the Christ. God wants our devotion, not our protection. As an educator, I believe truth is also quite muscular. It doesn't need our protection either. By faith, I believe when we stand with truth, we stand with God. So we must pursue truth, whether in the most cynical halls of our disciplines or in the hostile alleys of our culture. I doubted that I could be faithful to my professional convictions in a Christian college.

So as I considered Whitworth, I battled a bias. Most liberal arts colleges I knew were either suspicious of faith in their reverence of open-mindedness, or they frowned on open-mindedness in their protective attitudes toward faith. In choosing between the two imbalances, I had come to the conclusion that I would fare better as a defender of faith in a more liberal academic environment than as a defender of openness in a narrow Christian college's strongly conservative climate. A good liberal arts college needs a word from both Jesus and Bertrand Russell, and I decided I'd rather be where I was stumping for Jesus.

But as I looked at Whitworth, I was intrigued by what I thought I was seeing. The school seemed different from either of my two models. Somehow God's providence, deft leadership by the board, or dumb luck had endowed Whitworth with a fierce embrace of both Christian conviction and intellectual curiosity. I was astonished. I asked friends at Christian colleges what they thought about Whitworth. I loved it when I heard, "They're pretty liberal; they can't decide whether to be Christian or secular." Friends at secular schools also gave the right answer: "Great school, but very conservative; they can't decide who they want to be." The fact that Whitworth, like Bonnie and I, was Presbyterian put whipped cream on the situation.

When I arrived at Whitworth, my number one priority was to find out if the people really understood and loved this rare alchemy of conviction and curiosity. All the problems and opportunities could wait. I had moved a long way and passed on some pretty good situations primarily for a mission. I needed to confirm my hope that it was the real deal.

What I discovered thrilled me. The Whitworth community embodied this distinctive mission, but they weren't really aware of its gemstone value and didn't do a very good job of naming it. I had walked into a situation that was absolutely ripe for me to take a shot at transformation. The necessary components were already in place. First, the mission overlapped significantly with my deepest personal and professional values—I would never tire of promoting it. Second, this mission provided a very uncrowded market niche. Our faith emphasis put us on the right edge of secular institutions and even most church-related schools, while our fervent openness placed us on the left edge of Christian colleges. Third, Whitworth had underestimated its precious uniqueness.

My principal job as leader was to transform the way Whitworth College thought about itself, its mission and its potential. The energy with which I tore into this task rose from what I believed in my soul. If I was nothing else, I was authentic in declaring the worthiness of the Whitworth mission.

In telling my story I risk giving the terribly false impression that I am more noble than the next bloke, or that authenticity requires a mission of some glorious contribution to humankind. Neither is true. All I'm saying is that people in positions of authority have no chance of providing transformational leadership if they simply follow their noses to work every day, flip on the switch, say all the right things, then drag their fannies back home. As relief pitcher Tug McGraw chirped every time he opened his mouth during the fabled 1969 New York Mets march to and through the World Series, "Ya gotta believe."

I knew a guy in Pittsburgh who ran a company that made screen doors. You could not afford to ask him about those doors. If parents loved their children like he loved his metallic gates of splendor, it would be a better world. The man believed, and transformation cannot take place without that authentic leadership.

Authenticity is validated when people stand at close range. Observation is a greater power than overt persuasion. Said another way, a picture is worth a thousand words. When people see the depth of our convictions operating in everyday work, it turns up the volume on our claims. For me, leading from the middle accelerated the rate at which our people began to trust my efforts.

Adaptive: When Tom Matthews strode into town a couple of years ago, more than one of us had visions of a new sheriff. Donning a ready smile and wielding the reputation for a fast trigger finger, this Texan considered "business as usual" his #1 enemy. His new position as CEO of a big public utilities company put him in charge of the city's largest employer. With firmness and charm, Tom announced from day one that Washington Water Power, soon to take on the less regional name of "Avista Corp.," would adapt to the new economy or get eaten alive. Tom didn't much like the second option.

Transformational leaders all suffer from a touch of schizophrenia. Sometimes they respect history and deplore the present. They appreciate the efforts of their predecessors and they learn from the past, but they spit in the eye of the status quo. Other times, transforming leaders disdain history and relish the present. They bristle about their powerlessness over past performance, but squeeze every drop out of the present. Regardless of which side of the past-present disorder you bump up against, you will not find a satisfied bone in their bodies. They're always ready to adapt, to change. Never transformed, always transforming, these leaders are absolutely intolerant of inertia.

It was interesting running across Tom Matthews during his first year on the job. He actually broke the schizophrenia mold by grousing about both the past and the present. He would say to me, "Everybody tells me to slow down, but I feel like we're moving at a snail's pace." The poor guy was in such a hurry to get to the future that everything seemed slow to him. He came out of the chute slashing the company's stock dividend by 61 percent while chasing a few billion dollars in capital. He expanded operations into non-regulated, Internet-based markets and projected IPOs that he thought would spin back value to the shareholders.

Why was Tom in such a rush? Because he believed he was running a high-tech energy business, not a utility business. He knew that Avista could crank out profits for a few more quarters without major changes, but in this new world, the race to innovate was off and running. Tom had every intention of keeping his company, shareholders and himself in that race. Company efforts turned toward fuel-cell R&D, fiber-optic networks, Internet-based billing and calculating. Avista's employees joined Tom in thinking differently about the nature of the company.

Jack Burns observes "Adaptive action is not the characteristics or traits of a leader…(it) requires leaders and followers to participate in a process." Avista employees clearly "bought in."[5]

Unfortunately for Avista, the slope of its prosperity curve eventually turned sharply south, demonstrating the risk inherent in rapid precipitous adaptations. When Bill Gates picked up 5 percent of the company and Merrill Lynch analysts blessed it with a "strong buy" rating, Avista's stock volume exploded and its price tripled. Investors believed that "ol' Washington Water Power" had been transformed into an adaptive company, ready to parlay the next generation of high technology.

Well, they were wrong. Extraordinarily bad luck, and a couple of very bad decisions, ganged up to deliver Avista a big financial hit. Its stock price returned to the pre-Tom Matthews level, as the company was pummeled by astronomical year-2000 prices for the energy it had contracted to sell at a fraction of what it cost. When all this hit, Tom took responsibility. Although he could never have anticipated the skyrocketing price of energy, he was the leader, and bad stuff happened under his watch. Many Monday-morning-quarterbacks agreed with him when he accepted full responsibility for the problems. Eventually, Tom Matthews resigned under fire.

Some blame his style, while others blame his substance. But his successor, Gary Ely, and number-two person, Scott Morris, will say straight up that much of what Tom Matthews did had to be done, even though the particular adaptations turned out to be misdirected. My own opinion of Matthews' downfall is that he worked harder at adapting his company to the industry environment than adapting himself to the corporate and regional culture. Leaders must recognize that adapting their organizations to the environment depends on a series of corollary adaptations that can build support for change.

Being an adaptive leader doesn't always turn out rosy. It requires a stomach for risk, and as we learned from the technology companies that have been going under steadily since the turn of this century, risk is risky and change can be treacherous. But the 21st century will demand moves and counter-moves by its leaders. Leaders will adapt or be gone—maybe both—depending on how they go about it. But all organizations will lose ground in rapidly changing environments if their leaders are slow to adapt. Perhaps more than ever, leaders who can engineer successful adaptations will be in huge demand.

The danger of leading from out in front is that when we blow the bugle and yell "charge," we'll turn around and find no one following us. Adaptive leaders are particularly susceptible to this possibility. Adjusting our businesses to external opportunities and threats is often initiated by the leader, but it is never sustained without the front line people buying in. It is exactly when leaders are sizing up the environment and calculating adaptations that they become most vulnerable to losing touch with the warp and woof of their organization.

Many scholars have tried to decipher Sam Walton's formula for success. In a nutshell, the Walton family has converted good ideas into smooth running systems that are absolutely customer driven. But Sam Walton always knew that Wal-Mart's success rested on a workforce that kept up with his adaptations. The entire Walton family planted themselves in the middle of the business to lead and to listen through change. Noel Tichy observes that Sam Walton created a culture of "were-all-in-this-together" by naming and treating Wal-Mart employees as associates.[8] The Waltons simply could not have pulled off the kind of unity required for successful adaptations if they were detached from the organization. Sam Walton, one of the largest figures in business history, knew how to be just one of the "associates" when he was putting together a few stores in Arkansas. And he never forgot. He read the environment better than anyone in the industry, but he did his reading in the middle of his people.

Interactive: The leadership-theory folks seldom use the term "interactive" to describe the relationship between transformational leaders and the people they lead. "Mutual" or "shared" more frequently appear in reference to this tie. Generally, I would prefer an outcome term such as "mutual" to an input descriptor like "interactive."

One could argue that it doesn't matter how the leader and followers reach the mutual point of feeling that "we're in this together," but when it comes to leadership, I think it does matter. Profit sharing, employee stock options and employee ownership all build mutual benefit between management and employees, but they do not create transformations. People must feel engaged by more than structure. They need to feel a human connection with the one in whom they place their trust.

Six times each year I begin the day with all of our employees for a time of "inspiration, update, and questions." I try to create a spontaneous, interactive feel to the meetings. Our human resources director believes that those 20- to 30-minute meetings, preceded by coffee and fellowship, have created higher levels of confidence and trust in the administration than anything else we do. Although they use vastly different styles and methods, transformational leaders never lose contact with their people.

Those of us who live in the Northwest spin great Bill Gates yarns. We all know Microsoft employees and erstwhile employees (a.k.a. millionaires) who worked with Gates. One of my favorite stories I heard from a friend named Sam, who is also a friend of Gates's father. When young Bill came home for spring break during his sophomore year at Harvard, his father, Bill, Sr., asked Sam to talk some sense into his college kid, who wanted to drop out of school. Sam agreed and took Bill, Jr., out to lunch. After their two-hour meal, they shook hands and parted company. Sam walked straight to a pay phone and called Bill's dad, "Hello Bill," he said, "This kid doesn't need Harvard."

Whatever you believe about Microsoft, Windows, Bill Gates, or your Uncle Harry's gout, one thing you can know for certain: Bill Gates knows the Microsoft behemoth. One way or another, he pumps blood to every corpuscle of that company. It could be claimed that no one in history has done more to accelerate and expand human contact than Bill Gates. That's no accident; I think he created Microsoft just to keep up with himself. I'm not sure whether the Internet provides a metaphor for Gates, or if it's the other way around. The guy gives new meaning to the word "connected."

I had breakfast last year with a friend who recalled his first Bill Gates meeting as a Microsoft employee. Everyone knows that in your hour with the chairman the sin for which there is no remission is that of being unprepared. The mind facile enough to wing it with Bill Gates waits to be discovered. My friend, who was one of several people in attendance but not presenting, left the meeting absolutely stunned at Gates's performance. Every question Gates asked was perfect as he surgically disassembled and rebuilt the issues. The presenter had spent weeks preparing for his hour as navigator of the complexities. His job was to keep the chairman from any unproductive paths. Inefficiency steals the attention that interactive leaders need to give to the next issue. My friend reported that the meeting ended with a $100-million decision.

The legendary interaction stories of Bill Gates set a ridiculously high bar, but they do make the point. Transformational leadership skates along the ridge between empowerment and engagement. Leaders who empower but don't engage come across as disinterested. They rob group members of the leader's big-picture view. It feels like they've gone golfing while everyone else works. On the other side of the ridge, leaders who engage but don't empower feel paternalistic. Genuine interest can get interpreted as "checking up" or as a lack of confidence. Skillful interaction allows the leader to learn and advise without invading the delegated responsibilities of the team members.

In my judgment, maintaining a healthy ask/advise equilibrium is the most important balancing apparatus in walking the ridge. Transformational leaders both proclaim and procure information throughout the organization. I find it important to enter my all-staff meetings not only with information, but with at least one question. The symbolic value of this practice is good, but it runs a distant second to the real insight I gain from listening to employees' ideas. This balance between asking and advising or proclaiming helps establish the sense of mutuality that can transform the culture from being upward and downward into forward.

I have pretty good one-way communication skills, but sometimes they sit idle, waiting to be summoned by my not-so-great interaction sensitivities. Given the choice between the two, I'll put my transformation money on the leader with strong interaction patterns and modest speaking/writing communication skills over the leader with the opposite set. But whoever takes my bet is a sucker because a commitment to interaction builds communication skills. Furthermore, as interaction transforms the organization, messages get communicated by the culture as much as by pronouncements from the leader. This is why I consider the transformational model of leadership to be more anthropological than economic. The former communicates through high ideals and norms, while the latter communicates through exchanges and deals. Transformational leaders savor interaction with those they lead.

Leading from the Middle

It is in the middle of the people that leaders find the town square. From the pedestal interaction is rather challenging. To this screamingly self-evident observation, my younger daughter would add, "No duh." We need to be in the middle of the action if we are serious about expanding our interaction. Positioning ourselves can be as important as training in strengthening our interaction sensitivity and skill.

Transformational leaders in the 21st century will be the champions of progress because they are authentic, because they are willing and wise adapters, and because they will maintain high levels of interaction with those whom they lead. Public sentiment and, in extreme cases, government regulation will come down on the heads of manipulative leaders. The aftermath of self-serving executive financial packages and an impeached president will be a society that demands authenticity from its leaders. This same authenticity will position such leaders to exalt the values of the organizations they love and lead.

These leaders will also have the savvy, stomach and security needed to take on the adaptations required to stay relevant in a changing world. They will be paradoxical leaders that blend risk and wisdom in their campaigns. And certainly these transformational leaders will be donning their symbolic headsets, always interacting with their people and advisors. They will transform organizations into what James McGregor Burns characterizes as a "relationship of mutual stimulation and elevation."[7]

Chapter 17

Follower-Driven
Leadership

Transformational leadership ripples through an organization. To quote Burns, "Transforming leadership converts followers into leaders."[1] Empowerment acts as the electrical current in this conversion. Group members' motivation and commitment rise in proportion to their responsibility. They become transformers in the distribution of organizational energy. Confidence and accountability recharge group members as they take ownership of the vision.

To look only at the formal leader in a transformation model is to misunderstand the fundamental nature of this approach. Transformational leadership shifts the spotlight from individuals to relationships. Leaders' roles change, and they ask new and different questions. "Was I clear enough with Megan for her to get the job done?" is replaced by, "Do Megan and I have the kind of relationship that gives her the confidence to attack the job, but the security to ask freely for my advice?"

Transformation takes place through building and equipping, not assigning. Leaders who preach empowerment but horde leadership forfeit the credibility they need to serve as agents of transformation. They can't expect cartwheels from their people if the authority they distribute has a leash on it.

Sowing leadership throughout the organization presents one of the only moments when, in my opinion, ambiguity holds some value. A couple of years ago, I was fretting over all the stuff that didn't get done, or done well, for the imminent commencement exercises. After years of vowing, "I'm not going to let this happen again" caught up with me, I decided to take action. Noticing that most of the fumbles happened when I was carrying the ball, I knew it was time to yell for help.

Our capable new communications director seemed like the logical source of assistance. Between the time I made an appointment with him and the time of our actual meeting, I thought about where I needed relief. Initially, I thought about asking him to take the two specific jobs that I always botched up. Instead, I asked him to take leadership over all of my commencement responsibilities.

He accepted with great alacrity, saying he'd seen the responsibility coming. I offer this exchange as an example of when trading the clarity of a specific assignment for the more ambiguous "It's your baby" can have an empowering effect. I have to be willing to live with his decisions, and he has to be wise enough to know when to run something by me.

The idea of distributed leading is not new to the transformational model. In the 1950s, small-group theorist Robert Bales discussed various roles group members needed to play. He even suggested that groups need both a task leader and a relationship leader—usually two different people. But the difference between Bales' notion of roles and the way I think about the transformational model becomes clear when we think in terms of "leadership" rather than "leader."

Again, I'll appeal to my work group as an example. Our cabinet process is the product of climate control more than leader control or even role control. In other words, even though I move the agenda, I am not the source of social maintenance, challenges, innovation, or task drive. Furthermore, cabinet members have not assumed fixed roles in these process areas. Rather, the climate seems to beckon light-heartedness, task emphasis, calling for action, initiating structure, non-conformity, innovation and challenges at the appropriate times. Every cabinet member will deliver in each of these areas from time to time.

Leadership depends neither upon position nor upon role, but upon the seasoned instincts and wisdom of group members in a climate that signals people to step forward with what is needed. Granted, members vary in their comfort levels of providing the various kinds of leadership needed, but nothing in our process would suggest that role expectations limit individuals' contributions.

Setting the atmospheric conditions ranks as one of my most important jobs as the main leadership gardener. It's easier to do this with my immediate work group than with the entire organization, but it's no more important. One study found a significant correlation between the quality of leader-subordinate relations and subjects' satisfaction with the organization's climate.[2]

Clearly, the organizational culture influences the way people in line relationships view each other. In a tight hierarchical environment, superior-subordinate roles dominate people's perceptions of one another. That works well for certain groups, but for what I do, I'm shooting for a climate in which leadership is seen as qualitative—assumed according to need, rather than quantitative—assigned according to position.

Leaders need to think about what kind of culture will best cultivate leadership within their organizations, then put together a plan for making it happen. Edgar H. Schein suggests five opportunities for leaders to shape culture:
- Being selective about where they focus their attention
- Asking themselves how their reactions to crises will affect the desired culture
- Modeling the values they want to permeate the culture
- Rewarding desired values and activities
- Hiring and firing based on cultural expectations[3]

Each of these activities provides the leader with an opportunity to grow leadership throughout the organization. Too often we forget about the impact our decisions have on culture. I watched one of our vice presidents bring swift resolution to a stalled decision when I simply asked her what influence the retention or dismissal of an employee would have on the leadership culture within the institution.

Most leaders would benefit from mining the vast leadership resources buried within their ranks. Their organizations' leadership quotients would skyrocket if people looked at issues in terms of leading rather than simply executing. Those of us in the leader positions must provide rich soil for leadership to grow.

Transformational leadership is distributed and pervasive. It is not a finite commodity. When used, inventories replenish themselves with increasingly higher levels of quality. Transformational leadership is judged not by looking at the leaders, but by the quality and extent of leadership exercised throughout the organization.

Leading from the Middle

One day I took a break to run over and catch a swim meet on campus. Because this was a killer day work-wise, I had only about 40 minutes to give, so I had to make it count. The main folks I wanted to see were the swimmers, not only in their events, but between the immersions that would surely drown most mortals. As I was driving back home, I asked myself if my darting into the middle for a while did anything whatsoever to help our swim coach provide leadership. I did have the chance to mention how highly I regarded his work to three of our best swimmers; and I did have a chance to greet the coach and show him that I cared about his work; and I suspect I did have a chance to show swimmers and their families, friends and fans that I think what they're doing is important. So I think 40 minutes in the middle might have helped our swim coach a little in providing leadership to all the people he touches with his excellent work.

It may be wishful thinking to claim that we make our people better leadership providers by rubbing shoulders with them now and then. An argument could probably be made that we have the potential to intimidate or divert leadership when we enter the domains of our people. But precious few of the people we lead will claim that we diminish their leadership effectiveness with our presence.

If leaders hope to transform a culture, they must be willing to enter and affirm the colonies led by the people from whom they desire leadership. They must embody their expectations. Being an exemplar is tough to delegate.

Summary of Sections II, III, and IV

In these sections, I have presented the most enduring findings of leadership theory. Somewhat arbitrarily, I have divided this history into three periods. Theorists in the first era studied leaders searching for common traits that correlated with leadership effectiveness. For the most part, they considered these attributes to be inherent qualities rather than skills to be developed.

In the middle of the last century, theorists turned their attention from traits to the behaviors and styles that proved effective for leaders. They discovered not only that leaders differed in their preference of style, but that the effectiveness of different styles varied from situation to situation. Most of the studies related to style attempted to find out where a leadership style would fall on one of two continuums, then searched for various interaction effects between that particular style and a host of other variables. The two style continuums most frequently examined were autocratic vs. democratic and task-oriented vs. relationship-oriented. Predictably, schemes proliferated for identifying and developing leadership styles. Securing effective leaders became more complex than searching for the right traits.

The final phase of 20th century leadership studies focused on what theorists call transformational leadership. The transformational model rests on the belief that leaders can elevate individuals and groups to extraordinary levels of effort, nobility, and morality. As this transformation occurs followers are converted into leaders and the leader becomes the principal agent of inspiration and direction. The transformational leader will be most effective when he or she is authentic, adaptable and interactive. The leadership synapses in this model form in relationships and in organizational culture, making the leader one of several sources of direct leadership.

I offer two perspectives to the leader who desires to learn from this history. First, it is important to note that over the course of the past century, the general trend of leadership studies has shifted its focus from the leader to the followers. Early studies searched for the personal characteristics that made great leaders. Current thinking looks for leadership throughout the organization. The growing complexity of today's enterprises forces a diffusion of leadership. Today's leaders must not only provide leadership, they must create and inspire it in others. No longer will single sources of expertise, direction, information, and power be able to satisfy adequately an organization's needs to be responsive to changing environments. In other words, I'd rather find myself competing against the leaders who try to go it alone.

The second perspective I urge in looking at leadership history is one of respect. Even though today's experts present quite different views of leadership effectiveness than early researchers, the discriminating student will realize that current theories build on rather than replace past findings. In everything ranging from meeting new people to guessing on multiple-choice exams, experience teaches us to trust our first impressions. I have presented historical theories as trustworthy first impressions of the field. I encourage readers to learn from the durable insights found in leadership studies throughout the 20th century.

Section V
Changing Our Behavior

T wo nights ago a CEO friend of mine asked me what I was doing over the weekend. When I told him I was writing the last chapter of this book, he sighed, "The people who work for me love reading books on leadership, but I can't see where any of them are getting any better at leading anything."

Nobody has ever risen from being an ineffective leader to being an effective leader by reading a book on which steps to take. Frankly, that isn't about to happen to anyone racing to the last page of this book. Books don't change people—people change themselves through the decisions they make. Some great ideas about what changes we would like to make can be found in books, articles, speeches, counseling, and in a host of observations we make about the world around us. Personal growth is achieved through the discipline of our own decision-making.

This last section is less about becoming a better leader than it is about how people make significant changes in their behavior. Since we can't become better leaders without changing our actions, this section is worth reading. It is also worth reading because the approach to change that I'm suggesting can also help us change our behavior in every other area of life. I know this is big talk, but it works. I've seen it work with prison inmates, athletes, supervisors and CEOs. I've seen it work in my own life.

Having claimed that this section is worth reading, I admit that it is also one you might want to skip. First, it's advice won't work unless you do, and you'll really have to work hard to make it work. I am certain this section has the formula for a huge step up in the leadership effectiveness of most people. I've made it work for myself and I have seen it work in others. Anyone willing to commit to each component of comprehensive change can expect dramatic results. But the commitment is serious. Second, reading the theory in Chapter 18 gets a bit tedious, but it is important to understand why the formula works. I've tried to lighten it, but it's hard stuff to make titillating.

Finally, my discussions about change make a significant assumption. Although I recognize that we all have various assortments of quirks and dysfunctions, my suggestions are for what behavioral scientists would identify as "normal" personalities. Certain people have been damaged to the point of needing professional or medical assistance. I doubt if my prescriptions would be adequate in those cases.

Chapter 18
The Theory of Change

Simply *wanting* to be or do isn't enough. It never has been. You might want to eat less, exercise more, lead more effectively, and love your in-laws. But something happens between wanting and succeeding.

By my admittedly crude calculations, roughly 520 times between the ages of seven and seventeen I vowed on Sunday night that I would "be a better Christian this week." Simple vows would carry me through until mid-Monday morning. On those particular Sunday nights when I rededicated my life to God, I was a better Christian almost all day on Monday. If we had a special speaker plus I rededicated myself, my trend line didn't wilt until at least Wednesday. But I remember no Friday, in which I could detect any residual effect of my Sunday night guilt, shame and resolve. My weekly backslide became so regular that my attitude toward the Second Coming of Christ became "The earlier in the week, the better."

There's no doubt that my desire to be a good Christian was sincere, although painfully transitory. In fact, I majored in religion and philosophy in college, eventually going on to seminary. During those years, my understanding of faith grew at a faster pace than my stick-to-it-iveness, but both improved. Yet it was not until I turned from my theological studies and delved into the behavioral sciences that I began to understand just how complex and multifaceted life changes could be. At the master's level I studied the process of persuasion quite intensely, discovering that the meaning, origin and persistence of being persuaded varied greatly across people and circumstances. Although I became more intrigued with major life change, I was still pretty confused about where and when it would strike.

My first real understanding of "change" came during my last semester of doctoral classes at the University of Pittsburgh. I was enrolled in a social psychology research seminar where we studied attitude change. The text, by Martin Fishbein and Icek Ajzen, cited surprisingly discrepant findings in studies of the relationship between attitude change and behavioral change. The authors explained these inconsistent outcomes as the result of imprecise definitions of "attitude" and ambitious leaps from measuring attitudes to predicting behavioral change. In reviewing hundreds of studies, they found that researchers were defining any kind of pre-disposition toward an action as "attitude." Unless theorists looked at an entire group of these predispositions, they would find many unsupported hypotheses between an attitude and the behaviors they expected to follow. For example, during my "seven-to-seventeen years," a researcher could have asked me any of the following questions in search of my "attitude:"

- Do you think God is displeased when you use profanity?
- Do you think profanity is unbecoming to you?
- Do you like to use profanity to make a point?
- Do you ever feel good after using a bad word?
- Do you plan to stop using profanity?
- Are you intending not to say any bad words on Monday?

Some studies defined attitude so broadly that each of these six predispositions might have been used to represent my general attitude toward profanity. Not only was this an imprecise definition of attitude, it also implied that a hefty inference would be required to jump from the answer to any one of these questions to predictions about me cleaning up my mouth

Fishbein and Ajzen believed that a person's behavior was the product of an interaction among his or her beliefs, attitudes, and behavioral intentions. Basically, they claimed that beliefs represent a person's acceptance of information about an object or behavior. *Attitude*, as distinguished from the other two components, is evaluative or affective in nature. *Intention* refers to a person's plans to perform a particular behavior. Fishbein and Ajzen defined *behavior* as observable acts of the subject or person. In the profanity example, *beliefs* would refer to the first two questions (displeasing to God and unbecoming); *attitude* would refer to the second two questions (liking to use profanity to make a point and feeling good after using profanity); *intentions* would refer to the last two questions (not cussing on Monday and stopping altogether); and *behavior* would refer to acts related to profanity, such as cussing at friends, teachers, coaches and, of course, ministers.

In this example, Fishbein and Ajzen would confidently predict an end to my profanity if they found that I 1) started believing it was bad, 2) stopped enjoying it, and 3) planned to stop using it. They would be less confident in their predictions if they knew only that my intentions, for example, had changed and I planned to discontinue using profanity. Since researchers frequently measured only one of these three components, they often found an equivocal relationship between attitude change and a corresponding change in behavior.

In Fishbein's and Ajzen's scheme, beliefs generally exercised the most potent influence.[1]

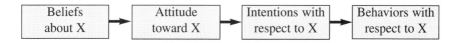

Underlying beliefs and attitudes, Fishbein and Ajzen believed *norms,* particularly those held by significant others, acted as influences that would kick in when it came time for the person to establish intentions with respect to the behavior. In my system, I see a broader influence than norms and have labeled it "environment." I have also treated "experience" with the particular behavior as an influence on the beliefs, attitudes and intentions related to the behavior.

The focus of Fishbein and Ajzen is on how beliefs, attitudes, intentions and behaviors are formed, as well as on how they interact with each other. Many theories and studies are examined from this perspective. They have written a wonderful text that has been a constant reference for me. But my interest, even as a doctoral student, has always been focused specifically on behavioral change.

Hence, I have used this theory as a foundation for different overall objectives than the principal ones held by the authors. That said, Fishbein and Ajzen do address "Principles of Change."[2] Their summary of research studies supports my claim that desire isn't enough. We can't assume that a person's change in attitude will be followed by a behavioral change.

Of all the issues studied by investigators in the attitude area, the question of attitude change has undoubtedly received the most widespread attention. The usual assumption is that by means of changing the attitudes of individuals it is possible to influence their behavior, to improve social relations or to produce social change.[3]

The authors, having demonstrated the inadequacy of changing behavior by changing attitudes alone, go on to make the strong point that beliefs and intentions must also support a change in behavior if it is to be predictable and enduring.

Perhaps it is because of my own frustrated attempts at controlling and changing my behavior that my personal study and research have focused on behavioral change. Frankly, I think this is a universal frustration to greater and lesser degrees. Even St. Paul, in the seventh chapter of his letter to the church in Rome, confessed, "Those things that I would, I do not; but what I hate, I do…. Oh wretched man that I am." I hear ya, St. Paul.

Is it primarily a lack of discipline that prevents us from acting in the ways we desire? Possibly, but I think it is more likely a tardy application of our discipline that leads to failed attempts at change. Certainly, discipline is a vital part of changing ourselves—we can't change without it—but we usually summon discipline to help us change when we're too far down the old road.

If we are to change our behavior, we need to change the causes of our behavior. To that end, I have been working toward a) understanding the relationship between behavioral patterns and what I believe to be the principal causes of behavior—beliefs, attitudes, intentions, environment and experience; b) examining how to work on these causes in a way that leads to a desired behavioral change; and c) engineering change in a way that gives it persistence.

The B-A-I-E-E-B model

A representation of what I believe to be the dominant influences on behavior would look like the following:

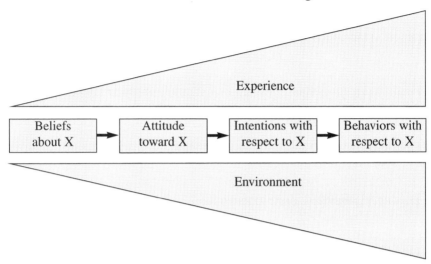

The angled lines encasing "experience" and "environment" symbolize the way in which the strength of these two influences grows as one moves toward the performance of a behavior. The well-known syndrome of what Irving Janis coined as "groupthink"—the reverence for unanimity—illustrates the power and progression of experience and environment over behavioral change.[4]

Janis goes into significant detail on how "groupthink" infected President John F. Kennedy's inner circle. He cites Arthur Schlesinger's reluctance, preceding the ill-fated Bay of Pigs invasion of Cuba, to voice dissent. The force of environment is clear in Schlesinger's lament, "I can only explain my failure to do more than raise a few timid questions by reporting that one's impulse to blow the whistle on this nonsense was simply undone by the circumstances of discussion."[5] Further, Schlesinger's experience with donning the prophetic mantle also discouraged him from dissent. He reports a private conversation in which Bobby Kennedy chided him, "You may be right or you may be wrong, but the President has made up his mind. Don't push it any further. Now is the time for everyone to help him all they can."[6] This self-censorship demonstrates how Schlesinger's past experience and the prevailing environment bore down to prevent a behavior that he believed was important, felt he should perform, and intended to do.

Definition of Terms

Because the purpose of this discussion relates to major changes in behavior, these definitions make no attempt to define terms in their broad sense, but looks at them only as they relate to a particular behavior.

Beliefs: the information, knowledge and conclusions that we assume to be true about a behavior.

Attitudes: our feelings about a behavior; liking, disliking, feeling good or bad about the action.

Intentions: our plans with respect to a behavior.

Environment: the context in which a behavior occurs and in which intentions, attitudes and beliefs are formed.

Experience: our past encounters with a behavior or issues and actions related to the behavior

Based on theory and supported by my experience, I have come to believe that our behavior changes to the extent that our beliefs, attitudes, intentions, experience, and environment propel the change. Here is a simple example that puts these five components of change in context:

> While Larry was faking enthusiasm in his annual review, his boss was faking satisfaction with Larry's performance. Weary with the dance, Larry blurted, "What do I have to do to get promoted?"
>
> His boss quickly replied, "Show some leadership!" In the honest conversation that ensued, Larry discovered that both his boss and his co-workers felt that he had often personalized issues in a way that caused him to be defensive and impaired his judgment. His boss reminded him how two weeks earlier she had told him that his department needed to come up with a plan to shorten the amount of time it took them to fill work orders for other departments.

220

He became very upset. He proceeded to give her concrete instances of how delays were not the fault of his department. Now, Larry's boss was telling him that his pattern of reacting to suggestions and requests made her fearful of promoting him.

"How are you going to improve if you interpret requests and suggestions as attacks?" she asked. "Frankly, we're able to get away with very few improvements to your systems because you've become so good at compensating for the process flaws. But at the next level, we need someone who can look objectively at the big picture and make it better."

Larry proved his boss's point by arguing that she didn't understand his area, and left the meeting upset with her. Later, Larry felt remorseful. This was not the first time his defensiveness had gotten him in trouble and he knew it. Larry wished he could change.

There are many different ways for Larry to go about changing this pattern of defensive response. But he needs to deal with all five components that influence his behavior.

Beliefs. Larry has been watching too much football. He thinks the best offense is a good defense. He must believe that suggestions and criticisms are opportunities to learn and to grow. He must believe that not all calls for improvement are personal criticisms. Unless he has evidence to the contrary, he must believe that people's motives can be trusted. He must believe that problem solving will produce better results than defending. He must believe that he holds greater job security in being open to feedback than in protecting himself.

Attitudes. This is a tough area for Larry. He feels rather heroic when he rises to his department's defense. Larry didn't get an A in debate by cowering from a challenge. He feels good carving up an opponent. Besides, Larry took a lifetime worth of crap from his "perfect" older brother; he doesn't need anymore from anybody else. But Larry needs changed feelings rather than hurt feelings. He needs to let himself enjoy the cooperative spirit of "Let's see if we can improve this." He needs to fear and repel the first signs of the defensive reactions that call him to combat. He needs to enjoy teamwork and welcome outsiders with suggestions as honorary team members. He needs a new attitude about feedback of any kind. He needs to love ideas for improvement.

Intentions. Larry is fun. He's spontaneous and loyal. He's a great friend. Unfortunately, spontaneity and loyalty conspire against Larry at work. Larry needs to get ready to change. He needs a plan. He needs to have clearly in mind how he will respond the next time he senses the first sign of criticism, feedback or suggestions for improvement. He needs some kind of an alert that will remind him NOT to do next what comes naturally. Initially, Larry needs an intervening device that reinforces his commitment to bring his behavior in line with his beliefs. He needs a set of specific intentions to break his pattern of defensiveness.

Environment. Larry knows there are certain circumstances that flip his switch. He is also aware that there are situations in which he has been generous in spirit. To whatever extent possible, Larry needs to engineer his environment so that he is responding in circumstances that support his desired behavior. Larry has discovered he benefits from a cooling-period. Because situations affect him so strongly, Larry has decided that stalling should be a part of his new pattern of behavior. In fact, Larry might do well to suspend his goal of non-defensive behavior and replace it with the more modest goal of muzzling his first response. Perhaps, as he becomes less defensive through the use of cooling-off periods, he can back off somewhat on delay being his first reaction. There is no dishonor in using crutches to help effect change.

Experience. Early in his career, Larry was burned by another person in his company whose advice he trusted. Since then, only the folks Larry knows well have been rewarded with his trust. This is where Larry should start. He should ask a reliable co-worker for suggestions on how he could improve his work. This would allow Larry to prepare himself to respond, and he needs a few early wins.

Psychologists call this *positive reinforcement.* Larry can be forgiven for some caution in the early stages of his efforts to change. It is important that his new behavior of openness be rewarded with a successful experience. This is where Larry's boss must be attentive to his desire to change. She must make him feel successful and protected when he lowers his fists and works cooperatively toward improvement.

This little example touches on a few ways in which Larry can work on each of these causes of behavior. However, the process is more complex and the causes run deeper than suggested by this quick fix for Larry. The following premises form the foundation of my system for changing behavior:

1. To change a pattern of behavior, one's beliefs, attitudes, intentions, experience and environmental influences must work together to support the change.

2. Erratic behavior is the result of beliefs, attitudes, intentions, experience and environmental influences moving in conflicting directions.

3. These components exercise influence over each other, sometimes in an overpowering way.

Not long ago, a discouraging report surfaced in which it was revealed that a group of teens, who had heard messages about the risks of smoking for several years, had picked up the habit at exactly the same rate as the control group that did not participate in the anti-smoking program. I wonder where the program sputtered. Perhaps the students believed all the health problems related to smoking were too far in the future to really matter. Or maybe the information wasn't convincing enough to overcome their "smoking is cool" attitudes. It could be that some kind of pledge not to smoke, similar to the kind of vow that some teenage sexual abstinence groups use, would have fortified their intentions. Perhaps when the students entered an environment in which the majority of students had not been indoctrinated, they just caved in to the social pressure. Or maybe these students had experienced homes and social circles where smoking was heartily approved. I'd love to read the researchers' assessment of why the program didn't work. I'd be willing to bet that a weakness could be found in at least one of these five areas.

As suggested in the "Larry" example, patterns of behavior change when all five of the components I've identified agree to work together (Premise 1). Occasionally, one or two components can out-muscle the others in the battle over behavior (Premise 3), but usually all five premises must come together for significant change. For example, when I was 30 a doctor told me I needed a healthier diet. What he said made sense to me (beliefs), and I really liked fruits and vegetables (attitudes). So I was in good shape on beliefs and attitudes. However, Bonnie and I didn't change our shopping patterns (intentions), I wasn't a pound overweight (experience), and I ate better than most of my friends (environment). So my periods of healthy eating were sporadic, with my beliefs and attitudes pointing toward carrots, and my intentions, experience and environment pointing toward ice cream (Premise 2).

At age 45, I discovered my cholesterol was up, my friends were starting to eat more wisely, and we started buying healthier foods. When my experience (cholesterol), environment (friends) and intentions (food purchases) came in line with my beliefs and attitudes, my healthy eating became a pattern rather than a rare token tribute to my internist's good advice.

As noted in Premise 3, sometimes one component can overpower the rest. I have a friend who learned after a check-up that his initial blood work had broken every cholesterol record in the Pacific Northwest. When he asked his doctor if they were going to put him on a treadmill, she gasped, "No!" and said he'd be lucky to make it to his car. Suddenly, his attitude, intentions and environment bowed quickly to his belief that cholesterol causes heart attacks and to his new information that he was experiencing a small city's worth of the stuff sludging through his arteries.

Perhaps the most important lesson to be taken from the three premises is that the key to a life change is that there is no one key. Major behavioral changes require major changes in the causes of the behavior. You can't pull off change by working only on one area. Many times I have responded to an article or speech on leadership with a new attitude or some new ideas, but seldom did I do the work necessary to change a pattern in the way I lead.

Unfortunately, we can't simply enter into a new understanding (beliefs) on how to be a better leader and assume we will therefore be one. We can't walk out of an inspirational management seminar pronouncing new excitement (attitudes) about being a good leader and assume we will therefore be one. We can't assume that if we make up one of those beautiful personal-growth plans (intentions), complete with a mission, strategies and tactics on being a better leader, we will therefore be one. Even if we have benefited enormously from the changes we have made (experience) and find ourselves working in situations that provide sufficient safety to make more changes (environment), the patterns of our leadership behavior won't change if we rely on only one of these factors to carry the load.

On the other hand, we *can* change if we are willing to work on each and all of the five causes of behavior. The good news is that a) tackling each cause breaks down the process of change into manageable tasks, and b) a new set of causes will have greater staying power than trying to discipline yourself without much support beyond "wanna."

Chapter 19
Six Steps to Successful Change

Julie Andrews was wrong. As much as I like *The Sound of Music*, the Do Re Mi tune gives bad advice. To "start at the very beginning" is *not* "a very good place to start." If we want to be better leaders, we need to start at the end result we're after, and then work our way back to "a good place to start." It won't work to begin with the question, "What beliefs do I need to be a better leader?"

The following steps suggest a process for making major changes in the way one leads. If it is followed, even the most stubborn behaviors can be reformed. Of the six 21st-century leadership qualities I discussed in the Section I, I have encountered one that, more often than the others, seems to make the difference between effective and ineffective leaders—communication. Many people with strong leadership potential have faltered because of ineffective communication patterns. So for purposes of illustration, I have chosen to use improved communication as the "end result" in which behavioral change is being sought in the examples that follow.

Step One: Self-assessment

I have a friend who confided in me his concern that he's too quiet around co-workers. "I'm trying to draw them out, sort of invite them to participate by my silence," he explained. Well, you'd have to administer smelling salts to his co-workers if you were to suggest this guy is "too quiet." He's developed the harmonica effect of talking both while exhaling and inhaling.

It is not possible to achieve the right results with the wrong goal. We must know our strengths and weaknesses in each behavioral area that we are trying to improve.

The ways in which we assess ourselves in a behavioral area differ little from the ways we assess an organization. Through a series of measures we identify perceptions of our strengths and weaknesses. Of course, ego plays a larger role in assessing ourselves than in assessing our organizations. It's risky to gather our colleagues' perceptions of our personal strengths and weaknesses, and then compare them with our own. We might end up with a bigger list of weaknesses than we're prepared to see. But it is essential if we wish to complete a successful change in behavior. As I have argued, beliefs form the foundation of our behavior. Our efforts will eventually crumble if our foundation is built using bad information. The inaccurate self-assessment of my loquacious friend will lead to an ugly awakening if he puts together a program to become more talkative.

Unless a person suffers from a psychological disorder, the primary tools needed to do good self-assessment are courage and honesty. To be sure, some very helpful instruments are available that can give feedback about one's leadership strengths and weaknesses, but I find their usefulness limited for two reasons. First, most of these tests measure our proclivities and preferences more than our capabilities and actions. Second, they often force their users into generic boxes that are not custom-made. I vote for the more primitive method of people sitting down with a legal pad and honestly recording what they feel are their strengths, weaknesses, likes, dislikes, accomplishments and failures in a certain behavioral arena. Having dealt with themselves, they then need the courage to elicit feedback from people in a good position to provide evaluations in the same areas.

I believe firmly that the fundamental awareness one needs to form a well-constructed behavior goal can be gained by courageously and honestly looking for it.

Self-assessment Example

Joan knew that organizational life in the 21st century would require effective communication from its leaders. She was bright, hard-working and confident; confident about everything except her communication effectiveness. She had come to this awareness reluctantly. Joan was a good speaker, initially masking to herself and others her shortcomings in other areas of communication. But Joan began to see that virtually every time one of her direct reports was upset, it could be traced to some kind of lapse in information that she should have provided. Joan decided to conduct an audit on her communication effectiveness. Here's what it involved:

1. She recorded all the specific instances in which she felt she had communicated effectively and those in which she felt she had been ineffective. She then wrote out a general evaluation of how well she felt she communicated.

2. She requested the same information from three of her direct reports, from three co-workers at the same labor grade, and from her supervisor.

3. She had asked a friend to pick three people from a list of seven and interview them about their "impressions of Joan's communication effectiveness." Her friend assured anonymity to the interviewees.

4. She identified congruencies in the evaluations and concluded that she was very effective when directly engaged, but she had a pattern of communicating too late, too narrowly, or not at all if she weren't asked directly for information. She was mortified to discover that within the organization she was considered a "weak communicator" who "keeps too much to herself."

Step Two: Goal-setting

Setting goals for changing a pattern of behavior is not the same as putting together performance goals for a MBO program. As it relates to leadership, goal setting for large behavioral changes is less scientific and more general. When someone pulls off a major change in the pattern of his or her leadership behavior, no one will need a calculator to verify the success. Changes of this magnitude are both self-evident and evident to others.

Good goals in changing a pattern of behavior should meet three requirements.

First, they must really be worth accomplishing. People who are willing to take on the big job of changing beliefs, attitudes, intentions, environment and behavior will lose their traction if they discover the goal won't deliver what they're hoping for, or that it isn't worth the effort.

Second, our goals must be within the right attainability range. When we build too much stretch into our goals, we have an excuse to give up by blaming our surrender on unachievable goals. On the other hand, goals that are too modest won't sustain our efforts. The meager magnitude of change fails to keep us motivated. We need attainable goals, but ones that require significant effort.

A few years ago I set for myself the goal of becoming a "teaching president." In addition to all the duties attendant to being a college president, I committed to do research, get current in my discipline, and teach a course every semester. Midway through the first course I agreed to teach, I found myself resenting my professional first love—teaching. Even though I had bent my beliefs, attitudes, intentions and environment into supporting this goal, I gave up. In retrospect, I wasn't changing my behavior as much as I was adding to it. My goal was too ambitious.

Third, our goals must be compatible with our basic genetic make-up. We can't change our DNA. When I announced five years ago to Bonnie that I was going to undergo a major personality change and become a safer, more conservative person, she laughed and said that she'd be satisfied if I just stopped picking up unsavory-looking hitchhikers. Changing a pattern of behavior is different than becoming a different human being. We need to set goals within the limits of who we are and what we have been called to do.

Good goals are ones that matter and ones that can be attained. We can change and improve the way we lead, and it's worth the effort. But trying to change our basic gifts or the fundamental duties of our jobs and lives will lead to frustration and failure.

Goals Example

Joan has decided to repeat her communication audit in one year. Her basic goals are for the three groups audited to a) make no reports of problems due to being left out of the loop or getting information late from Joan, and b) cite positive examples and general feelings that suggest Joan is on her way to becoming a "strong communicator." Additionally, Joan has set the goal of becoming "communication-conscious." In other words, Joan wants to keep her communication antenna up at all times, recognizing that her natural interaction patterns are too insular.

Step Three: Building Beliefs

When I was in my early 30s, I found myself failing miserably at every effort to change certain things in my life. My change model seemed to break down whenever it came time for the desired behavior. Finally, I reached the conclusion that I had some psychological defect, and I sought out a counselor. Although I'm sure I entered into counseling with a full complement of psychological disorders, my counselor startled me by suggesting that my failure to achieve the changes I was after was not a psychological problem. He delivered the news after I sighed, "Look, I just want my behavior to correspond to what I believe I should be doing."

His response was, "It does. You don't really believe you need to change." He went on to suggest that I rather enjoyed the way I was acting and in my heart and mind I didn't really believe my actions were all that problematic.

I'm not sure whether my counselor was completely accurate in his assessment, but he did make a point that I've never forgotten. Our deep beliefs are potent influences on our behavior. Fishbein and Ajzen claim that "the totality of a person's beliefs serves as the informational base that ultimately determines his attitudes, intentions, and behaviors."[1] Although I do not agree that beliefs are so deterministic, I do agree that they are *the* most powerful cause of the behaviors we choose. But I find it a bit misleading to picture one's belief system as the "origin" of attitudes, intentions and behaviors. If that were the case, we could focus exclusively on our information, knowledge and convictions, and assume the rest of the causes would fall in line.

For me, a better metaphor for the role beliefs play is that of a leader, with attitudes, intentions, experiences and environment all reporting to beliefs.

Using this image of beliefs as the leader or supervisor, we can categorize belief strength using various leadership typologies presented in Section III. I find the Tannenbaum and Schmidt's model works well in arranging the role and strengths of our various beliefs.

Teller beliefs. Our strongest beliefs, teller beliefs, tell all of the other causes of behavior to conform to their rule. For example, I believe intensely in the importance of leading with civility. It is a teller belief of mine, and it battles any signs of insubordination from my attitudes, intentions or environments. When I am unjustly accused and feel retributive, my attitude tries to get an exception from my belief in civility. Almost always, my civility belief will order my attitude back into shape.

Seller beliefs. Although these beliefs operate without significant alteration, they are not as strong as teller beliefs. They need to sell themselves to attitudes, intentions and behavior. I love watching two of our non-faculty co-workers when their seller beliefs are in action. In particular, these folks maintain the seller belief that shared governance is a necessary part of higher education life. They have seen the value of faculty governance in academic matters, but their attitudes run more along the lines of "butt out". Their minds are always trying to sell their attitudes on the notion that they should be happy that they don't have to mess around with all the academic issues. It's clear to me that their intentions, more than their attitudes, are obedient to this seller belief, as they ask faculty members questions and seek to understand academic processes. They also have enough belief strength to drag themselves into the prosaic environment of faculty meetings. Ultimately, their seller beliefs call the shots on shared governance, but these beliefs have to work hard when it comes to selling their convictions to their attitudes.

Consulter beliefs. This set of beliefs invites influence from attitudes, intentions, experience, environment and even our actions, but ultimately it supervises the other causes of behavior. It is in this category that Leon Festinger made a hit with his theory of cognitive dissonance. Festinger claimed it was quite natural to minimize the dissonance between what we believe and the actions we take or the attitudes we hold. We feel pressure to bring our beliefs closer to our actions, or vice versa. Aesop demonstrated this point when his fox concluded that the unreachable grapes were sour anyway. Entire libraries have been filled with research studies and hypotheses on cognitive consistency and dissonance reduction. Virtually all of this research would agree that tentative beliefs are more susceptible to change by our attitudes and behaviors than are strong beliefs.

For example, if I held civility as a "consulter" (tentative) rather than "teller" (strong) belief, it would exercise a less consistent influence on my behavior. Suppose I got caught off guard and snapped angrily at a student. If civility were a consulter belief, I might amend my beliefs to include exceptions for students, or for unusual circumstances, thus cognitively accommodating the behavior. The dissonance goes away as I change my beliefs. But if I hold civility as a teller belief, my logical response would be to maintain my conviction, apologize to the student, and work to keep myself from those "unusual circumstances." In both cases, my attitudes and intentions have to deal with my beliefs, but my consulter beliefs would be influenced more easily than my teller beliefs.

Joiner beliefs. These are beliefs that influence the way we think about behavior, but are not held strongly enough to stand up to strong challenges from attitudes, intentions and the environment. Recently, our college sought a government appropriation to establish a center for the study of poverty in our region. Proceeding with this requires my approval. In general, I don't believe that it's particularly smart for our government to use an appropriation system, and I would rather have some private donor give us the money. But my attitude toward the center's impact on the college and the region is very favorable; the project fits within our institutional plans (intentions); our congressman likes us and sits on the House Appropriations Committee and has worked hard on behalf of his district (experience); and the university down the street just got appropriation money for a center on environmental law (environment). So my beliefs about earmarking are not intense enough to exercise their authority over my attitude, intentions, experience and environment.

Thinking of beliefs as leaders of the other causes of behavior helps make two points. First, beliefs exercise a very strong influence over behavior and its causes. Second, beliefs vary in strength and type, as does their corresponding influence over the components of a behavioral pattern.

For us to execute enduring change in a significant pattern of behavior, we must have supportive beliefs and adequate belief strength. Or, to use the "beliefs as leader" metaphor, we need to have the right beliefs acting as tellers and sellers, supervising the other causes of behavior.

Beliefs Example

Joan's beliefs about her goal have already been influenced by the information she received from the communication audit. Before the audit, she believed that everyone has a bulging "to do" list and nobody needs or wants extraneous information. This belief diverted her from thinking inclusively about communication. She didn't want to bother people who were only indirectly affected by her activities. Joan also believed that when responding to others it was better for her to construct exactly what she wanted to say, even if it took a week or so, than to respond quickly and, perhaps, incompletely.

Now that Joan recognizes that her co-workers see her communication as usually too late and too limited, she has promoted three beliefs to "teller/seller" status: 1) It is absolutely better to err on the side of too much rather than too little communication; 2) It is absolutely better to err on the side of too many rather than too few receivers of her communication; 3) It is almost always better to provide fast responses with the admission that "These are my initial reactions, which may undergo some change," than it is to say, "I've spent the last several weeks considering this and here is my response." In other words, Joan must believe that responding at 65 miles per hour and 80 percent accuracy will be better received than responding at 20 miles per hour and attaining "perfect" results. Joan must also believe that her receivers will reward her efforts to be responsive with "accuracy grace."

Step Four: Shaping Attitudes

I think the most fundamental question about our attitudes is whether we choose them or they choose us. Do attitudes just descend on us, or do we have some choice in the matter? For a mood-swinger like me, the answer is easy. Other people choose their attitudes, but mine just overcome me. In other words, I can't help how I feel, but you can—so shape up. Most of us carry a double standard when it comes to attitudes, expressing scorn when we encounter the bad attitudes of others while hiding behind "I can't help how I feel" when looking at ourselves.

I realize that there are good people who do not enjoy a full range of choice. For some reason, their emotions have been damaged and they require psychiatric attention. But too often, those of us who are not emotionally impaired feel victimized by our attitudes. We grant them a sovereignty that renders us helpless. In one of the most supremely stupid lines ever uttered in pop music, Debby Boone wails, "It can't be wrong when it feels so right," and blah blah blah, "You light up my life." Not only do attitudes seem to overcome this singer emotionally, but they determine the morality of her relationship with whoever "you" is. Ms. Boone can't seem to help herself; she is surrendering to her attitude.

A few days ago I was going somewhere with my nephew, Tom, a very smart 30-something guy who also happens to be one of my best friends. Involved in his first really serious dating relationship, he's trying to figure out how two people can be both honest with themselves and sensitive to each other. He observed, "I don't want her to act cheery just because she thinks I need that, not if she doesn't really feel that way."

Actually, I think maybe he does want that. It's not a bad choice for her to make if she can put her mind in charge of her disposition without feeling phony.

Tom's observation makes two common assumptions about attitudes. First, attitudes just show up without being invited. We exercise little choice over how we feel. It's hard to know which side of the bed we'll wake up on. Second, it is natural and honest for us to act in accord with our feelings. To do otherwise is phony.

Good leaders do not accept either of these assumptions. Frankly, nobody should. They're false. People—at least those with non-impaired neurological, cerebral, and psychological equipment—exercise considerable choice over their attitudes.

I have a friend, Tanya, who is very happily married to a basketball coach who travels a lot. He and I talk regularly, so I know when he's out of town. A year ago I decided to call Tanya while her husband was gone, just to see how life was treating her, and to cheer her up. When she answered the phone, it sounded like a rock concert was going on in her lap. The screams, shouts, and bursts of laughter competing with my "Tanya, is that you?" were the normal sounds of her three little rug rats going crazy. When I yelled the question, "How you dealing with everything, Tanya?" no decibel level could have drowned out the power of her response. "I'm doing great, Bill. I don't have any choice."

As a matter of fact, Tanya was doing great because she *did* have a choice, and she made a healthy one. She chose to accept the steady chaos that comes with the high calling of being a parent and the principal support person for the four other people in her family. Having accepted that choice, she then chose happy and upbeat over whiny and frustrated, knowing that a nasty attitude would not improve the physical circumstances of her life one iota. So Tanya *chose* to be happy. She rejected the role of victim. She chose the role of victor.

The research in attitude formation is pretty complicated. Behavioral scientists are sometimes guilty of attempting to explain and predict human behavior using formulas and tools borrowed from natural scientists. On the other hand, former behavioral scientists like me tend to oversimplify our explanations for why people act and feel as they do. True to my own characterization, I would like to make the argument that, in general, attitudes are formed and changed by associating what we believe (including information we have) with a particular object or behavior.

When I was seven years old I went to my first major league baseball game in Chicago's Comiskey Park. It was there, worshipping my summer gods in their white wool uniforms, that I smelled my first cigar. To this day, I love that smell. It is the romantic smell of baseball on 35th and Shields.

Attitudes are so much the products of our associations that sometimes even what would naturally feel bad feels good to us. For example, most of the time we have a negative attitude toward pain, but by association our attitude toward pain under certain circumstances can make it feel wonderful.

Much of what experience has taught me about attitudes has come in the athletic arena. To preserve relationships, I have been forced to choose attitudes that don't come naturally. For years, my friend, Pat Cunningham and I engaged in epic tennis and racquetball battles. They would end with the two of us sprawled on the court, totally spent, while pain shot through our shoulders like a thousand needles.

At that moment of exhaustion and finality, the loser despised both of us as he recited, again, the litany of how pathetically he'd played and that surely this was the last time he would ever play this stinking sport. But for the winner, pain was the welcome messenger that reminded him of the glories of sport and the goodness of this friend heaped along side of him—this friend who on this day hated his guts.

Today my attitudes involving direct, physical competition are profoundly affected by the wars with Pat and all the other good friends with whom I've competed. The associations are so strong that when my nephew drills me in a set of tennis, the loss feels not so much like one set as like the accumulation of every set I've lost in my entire life. If I'm not careful, I will associate one event with thousands and let the feeling crush me. But I have come to realize that I don't have to bear emotionally all the losses of my life with every new loss. If I prepare myself to respond with new associations, I loosen myself from the emotional tyranny of negative associations.

Some time ago, I was at the gym with my son, shooting baskets. After he threw down two dunks and several three-pointers while I was doing stretching exercises that would put me in a position to tie my shoes without assistance, he offered to play me in one-on-one. For his first 20 years, which were my years 30 to 50, I owned this boy in one-on-one. Even a year or two after he had the skill to beat me, he either lacked the mental toughness or he else he realized it was better for our relationship for the less mature one of us (me) to win. But I am not a stupid man, and it was clear to me that this was his day. No matter how wily, crafty and whiny I might be, the time had come when he would find consummate joy in destroying me. And destroy me he did.

But before he did, even before we started, I was frantically disassociating all the losses in my life from the one I knew I was about to have administered. I needed to associate this imminent loss with all the wins of being Ben's dad. It worked. As I crumbled to the floor, gasping after my barrage of fouls failed to prevent the inevitable, I crowned him the new king of one-on-one, winner-whenever-he-wanted-to-win, and it felt good.

I have discovered that I can go through the same kinds of preparations that lead to the creation of positive associations with leadership patterns that are important but that I don't particularly like. For years I dreaded doing my monthly newsletter. I would have abandoned the practice, but folks seem to really like it. A couple of years ago I realized that I needed to change my attitude toward this discipline or I'd start writing it poorly while it drove me nuts. To that end, I met with the folks who sent me information, my assistant and proofreader/editor. I told everyone what I liked least about writing this thing. What surfaced was that "writing" was the one thing I did like. The components of my dread turned out to be the organizing, searching for incomplete information, waiting for late information, and patching writing time into my schedule. So now, my assistants get everything ready, including a chunk of uninterrupted time. When I wake up to a "write the 'Mind and Heart'" morning, I make a pot of coffee and sit down in a good mood, ready to go...usually.

As I said above, attitude formation is very complex, and there are many points that could be made about its nature. For the purposes of this discussion on implementing new leadership behaviors and patterns, the two most important starting points are 1) rejecting the notion that we are victims of our feelings, and 2) engineering our circumstances and preparing our thinking to make positive associations with our desired behaviors.

Attitudes Example

Joan is strong and efficient. She doesn't waste many moves. If she is a bit slow in responding to her direct reports it is because she's going to get it right the first time. She also finds it irritating to spend time keeping folks in the loop if they are not directly affected by the information. Joan is a pleasant person, but she's pretty much all business, and she wants to set that kind of example for her people. She has an open-door policy, but only folks who want information from her should use it.

Joan needs to build a positive association with the communication pattern that has become her goal. Achieving her goals while hating the behavior will consume too much emotional energy. Currently, she associates frequent and broad communication with lost time and productivity, although she recognizes that the people she leads find her insular.

Joan can create a positive association with her new desired behavior by connecting it to something she values and enjoys. It might be a pleasant team meeting, or, perhaps, Joan's secretary needs to block a weekly hour when they duck out for "coffee and communication." Joan could automatically include her secretary on all e-mail items, and then when they get together for their coffee-and-communication hour, Joan's secretary could raise a series of "How can I help you with this item?" questions. Joan needs to convert a negative feeling toward a behavior by attaching that behavior to something she values and enjoys. The "something" will be up to Joan to discover.

While getting our beliefs of how we need to change to our desired changes in behavior, attitudes will either propel us toward our goal or fight us at every turn. Without supportive attitudes, all that's left to help us change is force. Either the force of circumstances or the force of our self-discipline will need to muscle us toward our goals. We know from all of our lapses in discipline that attitudes, what we like and don't like, will win its fair share of battles. For this reason, we must not accept negative attitudes toward what we believe is right. We can choose to shape new attitudes through new associations. Doing so will certainly boost the odds of achieving our goals.

Step Five: Organizing Intention and Environment

Although our intentions play a different role than our environment in bringing about behavioral change, I have chosen to treat these two influences together because they are both managed through planning. As previously stated, intentions refer to our plans with respect to a particular behavior. Environment refers to the context in which a behavior occurs.

Often, we just expect our behavior to change in concert with changes we make in our beliefs and attitudes. If we make no changes in our lives to support what we believe and feel, the "round hole" of our habits and surroundings will reject the "square peg" of this new behavior we're after. I can recall in the late 1980s coming to grips with the impact that my romance with tradition was having on the adaptability of the institution I was leading. I had good marketing instincts, but they were bound by my skepticism of all things new. I liked classical music, classical literature, classical clothing and classical colleges. I was not into "hip." So I vowed to become a more current leader, and I began to read books and articles on innovation. Along with my growing knowledge was an excitement I felt about getting closer to the cutting edge of things. I was putting together a new self-image. I was on my way to being contemporary. But I had neither support nor accountability to keep me on track. I simply tried to will my way into providing a different kind of leadership, and it wasn't long before the routines of my job nudged me back into the deep grooves of my old ways.

Many social psychologists have discovered that people often fail to make desired changes in their lives because they have not planned and organized for change. They have falsely assumed that once beliefs and attitudes are headed in the same direction, behavior will automatically follow. One of the best ways I have found to calculate what I need to do with my intentions and environment is a variation on Kurt Lewin's force-field analysis. The model is pretty simple, consisting of four components, but strategies and executions are never simple. The components are:

- the desired behavior—your goal;
- an accurate assessment of your current behavior with respect to the goal;

• all the forces that propel your current behavior toward becoming your desired behavior;

• all the forces that prevent your current behavior from becoming your desired behavior.

In constructing a force-field analysis, it may be worthwhile to break down the propelling and preventing forces into beliefs, attitudes, intentions and environmental factors. I have found, however, that the exercise is most helpful in calculating the impact of environmental influences. Hence, I have included this assessment tool in the "intentions and environment" discussion.

Intentions and Environment Example

The benefit of constructing a force field analysis becomes clear if we return to Joan's goal of becoming a more effective communicator. One of Joan's direct reports observed, "Joan communicates with me only when a direct response from me is required or when I have communicated directly with her. This leaves me and others out of the loop on information that is relevant and helpful." Joan has painfully accepted this as a representative perspective of those with whom she works. She has decided she wants to deliver weekly "FYIs" to various people and groups.

Five forces are propelling Joan toward her goal of communicating information of interest and relevance weekly: 1) she likes those with whom she works; 2) she has a very organized secretary who prods her; 3) she frequently works electronically; 4) she is quite multitasked; and 5) she is a good communicator when engaged.

However Joan also faces six powerful preventing forces: 1) she has an erratic schedule; 2) she is too busy; 3) she is uncertain about what information is needed; 4) she has a personal disdain for superfluous information; 5) she isn't near those who desire the information; and 6) she faces countless distractions.

As a result of these competing forces, Joan currently communicates with others infrequently and non-punctually. She puts her head down and plows forward, providing others with information only when necessary.

If Joan is to reach her goal, she needs intentions that will position her to succeed and an environment that will support her efforts. Because she has done good work on building a foundation of supportive beliefs and attitudes, Joan can focus her strategy for change on intentions and environment.

Strategy for Change

We can use the force-field analysis to build a three-part strategy for change:

Step 1: Weaken the forces of resistance. Joan must attempt to eliminate, offset or disempower each preventing force.

Step 2: Strengthen the forces of propulsion. Joan needs to identify ways to fortify each of the forces that push her toward the goal.

Step 3: Integrate the analysis into a strategy. If Joan were to come up with the following strategy for achieving her goal, she would neutralize each preventing force while exploiting each propelling force:

• Joan's secretary will block out a "communication hour" every Monday or Tuesday. She and Joan will forward their phones, get their favorite coffees, and focus on two tasks. The first task will be to specify the information Joan needs to communicate electronically with various people. The second task will be to identify the people Joan needs to contact directly.

• Between meetings, Joan and her secretary will both keep close watch for information that would be helpful to co-workers. They will both create electronic files entitled, "communication meeting" into which they can drag various items for discussion and possible distribution.

• After the meeting, Joan's secretary will draft the electronic messages and send them to Joan for editing and distribution. She will also put electronic reminders on Joan's computer to contact directly the specified people.

• Monthly, Joan's secretary will add an hour to Joan's team meetings. During that time Joan will report on her most important projects and respond to questions from her direct reports. The others will do the same as time permits.

If Joan implements this strategy, she will have compensated for all of the preventing forces while taking advantage of all the natural influences that move her toward being the communicator she is dedicated to becoming. By programming her intentions and engineering her environment, Joan has a strategy that promises success. It will be a team effort with her secretary, and that will help significantly by structuring accountability into the process.

In altering our leadership patterns, working on intentions and environment could be characterized as the blocking and tackling of change. It lacks glamour, frankly. Often we find our beliefs and attitudes changing on the mountaintop of a great conference or when we are lifted by witnessing a great leader. But these internal changes that occur high above life eventually collide with the street-level influences that molded the old behavior that we would like to change. Various influences contributed to the patterns we have established and will try to keep us in those patterns. Old wineskins will hold the new wine of change for a short time before they burst. It takes hard work and discipline to build a personal and organizational framework in which the inertia that binds us can be conquered.

Step Six: Using Experience

From time to time, we all hear mental tapes of the lives we've lived. Some tapes make us smile, while others put beads of sweat on our brow. Some tapes are dangerous, but most are not. In fact, remembering is largely helpful, and we can use memories to support desired changes in our lives. I am quick to admit that some past experiences are best dealt with professionally. Psychologists can help us find the "play" buttons for recordings suppressed or long forgotten, and sometimes they help us hit the "stop" button, or at least to change tapes. This work is important, but I believe strongly that most people are not shackled by most experiences. In other words, we have the potential to loosen the drag created by negative experiences and to create new experiences that support change.

A good way to look at the impact that experience exercises over our efforts to change is again from a force-field perspective. In considering a new behavioral pattern, one should ask a) what past experiences will discourage this particular change? b) what past experiences will encourage this change? and c) what new experiences can be created that will encourage this change?

The benefits of this analysis lie largely in predicting the outcomes of the change we're seeking. If the change we're contemplating is largely supported by past experience (a > b), we'll have confidence when it comes time to act. If, however, there are more negative experiences associated with the new behavior we seek (a < b), then we can predict a tougher time converting beliefs, attitudes and intentions into behavior. Also, analyzing a and b will help in the identification of new, reinforcing experiences as a part of the overall strategy for change. In virtually all areas of change, early wins are extremely important reinforcement measures.

Recently the parent of a student questioned my leadership because I wasn't doing enough with respect to a situation that we agreed was bad. He wasn't aware of all that I had been doing, but I think he had a point. I wasn't being as aggressive as I needed to be in this personnel-related matter. I hated to admit it to myself, but I realized that I had become less aggressive than I once was. My current proclamations of the wrongdoing I see have become safer.

One of the most stirring points of my acceptance speech as board chair of the Spokane Regional Chamber of Commerce was when I proclaimed poverty as hurtful and wrong. My passion was inspiring, but safe. None of the 1,500 people present came up after the meeting and tried to claim that poverty was a good thing. I don't deserve any courage points for that.

One of my goals in the years ahead is to use my formal and informal power to stand against what I believe is wrong. In thinking about this goal, I have found it helpful to reflect on how past experience has affected my nerve. What in my experience has reinforced my efforts to take moral stands? What has discouraged me from taking moral stands? What tapes are being played in my mind when I face something I believe is wrong?

When I analyze my past experiences, the risk-reward ratio tells me to look at the forest. It's growing well. Do I really want to take on the trauma of chopping down a few morally diseased trees, especially when some of the other trees disagree sharply with what I consider to be a moral disease?

Regardless of what I hear on the old tapes, the answer to this question must be "yes" when I'm dealing with moral conflicts. I have five questions that I try always to ask whenever I feel conflict of any kind.

1. Is there a win-win resolution to this conflict?
2. If not, can I simply accommodate the position that is different from mine?
3. If not, is there a compromise that will provide partial satisfaction for both sides?
4. If not, is this conflict worth resolving, or is the solution more costly than living with the problem?
5. Is this a moral issue requiring a "win-lose" resolution?

Whenever I answer "no" to the first three questions and "yes" to questions 4 and 5, I must act. But I must also understand that taking action on moral grounds will trigger flashbacks that can steer me in the opposite direction.

Drawing on my past experiences with morally driven decisions, I have built a strategy for renewing my aggressiveness in this area. Whenever I'm faced with an opportunity to exercise moral leadership, I create a microcosm of the larger group that would be affected by my actions. The core of this representative group is the president's cabinet, but I almost always consult with people beyond those who report to me. I am pretty specific in addressing each of the preventing forces that discourage me from taking action. Having the opportunity to discuss the inevitable challenges hones and broadens my thinking while giving me a better feel for the magnitude of the reaction I can anticipate. These discussion groups have also helped reinforce my propelling experiences by identifying the benefits of past morally based actions.

Actually, I found myself in the midst of using this strategy on a huge issue last year. Our campus was wired with total access to the Internet on all college computers, as well as on the personal computers in all the residence-hall rooms. Regrettably, we received way too many self-reports from students that pornography was taking an evil grip on their time and thoughts. Because more than once I had failed to resist pornography when it was readily accessible, I voiced many deep concerns about this issue when we were wiring our residence halls for the Internet. I ended up accepting the arguments that there are more developmentally beneficial ways to help students resist pornography than using the rather indiscriminate filters available at the time. Several years later, we had to admit that our "developmentally beneficial" ways of discouraging misuse of the Internet did not seem to be working for a lot of guys on campus.

I decided to study this issue and make a decision about whether to impose filters. Either change or maintaining the status quo would be an undeniably moral action, made particularly complicated by the fact that arguments both for and against filters have the same moral foundation. At the core, the argument is loss of control versus loss of control. One group feared losing control of free inquiry and basic First Amendment rights. The other group feared losing control of their inner lives in a way that could eventually work its way into hurtful actions.

My strategy of building the microcosm and moving outward seemed to work. The groups I assembled gave me insight on the issue, courage to act, and confidence that I was on the right course. In the cabinet we discussed the negative and positive experiences of the last time I took on a tough moral issue, and it was extraordinarily helpful in heading off hurtful responses. I also convened "town meetings" with students, faculty and staff. They raised questions and made comments that I never would have considered. In the end, we made a good decision that was surprisingly well received.

Perhaps the most important gift presented to us by past experiences is a sharpened sense of anticipation. For us to neither listen nor learn from the past will condemn our actions to being underinformed and to the dreaded prospect of history repeating itself. We will replace studied understanding with instinctive optimism or pessimism. Clearly, we should listen to our gut instincts, but they should be given authority only after we have examined the experiences that formed them. We have no choice in whether we are influenced by experience. We are. Our choice is in how we learn from those experiences to make us more effective in our leadership.

Summary

A couple of days ago I sat with a prospective student who'd spent his first two years of high school off on some strange social and pharmaceutical adventures. Whatever "messed up" means, he fit the bill. My young friend had taken a fast track to hell and had little hope of outgrowing his condition. His only chance for reform was an incredibly intense new belief, new attitude, new intention, and new environment. Because of his age and situation, salvation was initiated in the form of an intensely different environment (an isolated rehabilitation school) and then worked its way inward.

Beliefs, attitudes, intentions, environment and behavior seldom come in equal strengths. Major changes in a person's behavioral pattern can almost always be traced to an intense change in one (initially) or more of the components that determine behavior.

The relative influence of beliefs, attitudes, intentions, environment and experience on one's behavioral patterns will be influenced by the strength of each component. Our attempts to make significant changes in basic behavioral patterns of leadership must take into consideration different levels of intensity in the influences that lead to our actions. If we are going to take on the hard work of change, we will do well to identify whether beliefs, attitudes, intentions or environment will do the heavy lifting for us. We can then invest our efforts in the most likely area of influence.

The question every leader must ask is whether change is worth the effort. For me, going through the process of change has been enormously gratifying. Dealing with each component has been far more enriching than onerous. Learning, renewing my spirit, reforming my plans, and restructuring my environment have all rewarded me, independent of the changes they have produced in my leadership. Beyond my renewal and enrichment, I know that students, employees, alumni and friends of the college have a better leader than the one who was cruising on automatic pilot. Their affirmation, more than anything else, gives endurance to these new leadership patterns.

I remember seeing in Gary Larson's wonderful "Far Side" cartoon calendar a picture of a deeply worried-looking dog, inching forward on a tight rope. In a bubble above his anxiety-stricken expression was the caption, "I'm an old dog, and this is a new trick."

At times, change feels just that way, but we can make it across the tightrope. The benefits on the other side will make us—and those whom we lead—glad we accepted the challenge.

Epilogue

The world has changed since I finished writing this book. Two days ago I handed diplomas to over 400 eager graduates. Today the morning newspaper headlines announced that the next chapter of "911" would be suicide bombings on U.S. soil. What will become of the hopes and dreams that college degrees are supposed to deliver?

Fear seems to centralize leadership. In the months immediately following September 11, Americans seemed anxious to put their futures in the hands of President Bush. As a baby boomer, I remember a similar sentiment in my dad's assuring words that "Ike" would get us through the cold war. Ironically, the best response from a central leader whose power has been boosted by external threat is to give it back to the people. This country needs "we the people" leadership. We need leadership in every business, borough, airport, and household in America. President Bush, and all of us in positions of responsibility, need to heed the advice of James McGregor Burns and convert followers into leaders. Leaders building leaders is our only hope for the exponential rise in leadership we so desperately need.

A couple of nights ago as I was preparing to tackle a very difficult threat to our campus, I found myself thinking about how much i love the rush of rallying our people. I thought about how listening to students, faculty, and staff gives them power and me wisdom. I thought about setting a tone for this difficult challenge we face. I thought about how much easier it is to write about leading than to do it. I thought about how much more satisfying it is to do the work of leadership than to write about it. So, let's get back in the middle of our people and lead them well. May God give us the strength to infuse them with the wisdom, power, and confidence needed to fulfill the high calling of leadership.

Notes

Preface

1. Burns, James MacGregor. Leadership. (New York, NY; Harper Torchbooks, 1978).
2. Rost, Joseph. Leadership for the 21st Century. (New York, NY; Praeger Publishers, 1991).
3. Kelly, George A. A theory of Personality. (New York, NY; The Norton Library, 1963).
4. Rost, Joseph. Leadership for the 21st Century. (New York, NY; Praeger Publishers, 1991).
5. Burns, John S. "Defining Leadership: Can we see the forest for the trees?" The Journal of Leadership Studies. Vol. 3, No. 2, 1996.

Introduction

1. John 1:14
2. Fishbein, Martin & Ajzen, Isek. Belief, Attitude, Intention, and Behavior. Reading, MA; Addison Wesley, 1975).

Section I

6. Rost, Joseph. Leadership for the 21st Century. (New York, NY; Praeger Publishers, 1991).

Chapter 1

1. Handy, Charles. Beyond Certainty. (Boston, MA; Harvard Business School Press, 1996).
2. Handy, Charles. Beyond Certainty. (Boston, MA; Harvard Business School Press, 1996).
3. Bennis, Warren. Old Dogs, New Tricks. (Provo, UT; Executive Excellence Publishing, 1999).
4. Gerstner, Lou. "A Policy of Restraint," Leadership Magazine, vol. 3, No. 2.
5. Drucker, Peter. Forbes, 3-10-97.

Chapter 2

1. Cronin, Thomas & Genovese, Michael A. The Paradoxes of the American Presidency. (New York, NW; Oxford University Press, 1998).
2. Cronin, Thomas & Genovese, Michael A. The Paradoxes of the American Presidency. (New York, NW; Oxford University Press, 1998).

3. Cronin, Thomas & Genovese, Michael A. The Paradoxes of the American Presidency. (New York, NW; Oxford University Press, 1998).

4. 1 Corinthians 6:9-10; 12:10.

5. The Economist. September 1996.

6. Proverbs 29:18

7. Tichy, Noel M. The Leadership Engine. (New York, NW; HarperBusiness, 1997).

8. Bennis, Warren G. & Nanus, B. Leaders: Strategies for Taking Charge. (Hew York, NY; Harper & Row, 1985).

Chapter 4

1. Kouzes, James M. & Posner, Barry Z. The Leadership Challenge. (San Francisco, CA; Jossey-Bass, 1997).

Chapter 6

1. Burns, James MacGregor. Leadership. (New York, NY; Harper Torchbooks, 1978).

2. Kellerman, Barbara & Matusak, Larraine R. Cutting Edge: Leadership 2000. (College Park, MD; Center for the Advanced Study of Leadership, James MacGregor Burns Academy of Leadership, 2000).

Section II

1. Yukl, Gary A. Leadership in Organizations. (London; Prentice-Hall International, 4th Ed., 1998).

2. Bass, Bernard M. Handbook of Leadership. (New York, NY; The Free Press, 1991).

3. In 18 of 23 studies reviewed by Bass and Stogdill, the average leader did test to be more intelligent than the average member of his or her group. However, in five of the stud ies, too much intelligence proved to hurt the leader's ability to lead the group.

4. Rost also holds this point of view; citing four major studies conducted in the 1980s that he argues were, in essence, dressed-up versions of trait theory (p. 28).

Chapter 8

1. Yukl, Gary A. Leadership in Organizations. (London; Prentice-Hall International, 4th Ed., 1998).

2. Bass, Bernard M. Handbook of Leadership. (New York, NY; The Free Press, 1991).

3. Kouzes, James M. & Posner, Barry Z. The Leadership Challenge. (San Francisco, CA; Jossey-Bass, 1997).

4. Bass surveyed the research between 1948 and 1970, he found "25 studies-—many more than the 1948 survey which suggested that the leader tends to be endowed with an abundant reserve of energy, stamina and ability to maintain a high rate of physical activity" (p. 81).

5. Shields, Mark "Wanted: A Gipper for the Democrats," The Washington Post. December 3, 1985.

Chapter 9

1. Goodenough, F.L. "Inter-relationships in the behavior of young children," Child Development, 1, 1930.

2. Asch, Solomon. "Forming impressions of personality," Journal of Abnormal and Social Psychology 1946.

NOTES

Section III

1. Clearly, patterns of approaches to leadership emerged in the seminal studies in the 1950s. For example, in the Big Ten alone, leadership studies at Ohio State (Halpin and Winer, 1957), Michigan (Katz and Kahn, 1952), and Illinois (Fiedler, 1953), were finding research value in dividing leadership approaches into "task" or "relationship" patterns.
2. Bales, R. F. Readings in social psychology. (New York, NY; Holt, 1958).
3. Chapter 10 of Gary Yukl's Leadership in Organizations gives an excellent overview of the five dominant style-situation theories.
4. Lewin, Lippett, and White, "Patterns of Aggressive Behavior in Experimentally Created Social Climates." Journal of Psychology, 1939.
5. Likert, R. New Patterns of Management. (New York, NY; McGraw Hill, 1961).
6. Tannebaum, R. and Schmidt, W.H. "How to Choose a Leadership Pattern." Harvard Business Review, 36, 1958.
7. In the known world's most comprehensive compilation of leadership studies, Handbook of Leadership (1991), even Bass entitles the chapter on these studies, "Task- versus Relations-Oriented Leadership." The only lower case word in the title, "versus," reveals the way most researchers look at the relationship between these two variables.

Chapter 10

1. Likert's typology, (Authoritarian, Benevolent Authoritarian, Consultative, Participative), sneaks in a value-laden adjective when distinguishing between "Authoritarian" and "'Benevolent' Authoritarian" leadership.
2. DePree, Max. Leadership Is an Art. (New York, NY; Doubleday, 1989).
3. Janis, I.L. Victims of Groupthink (Boston, MA; Houghton Mifflin, 1972).
4. Kilman, Herbert. "Compliance, identification, and internalization: Three processes of attitude change." Journal of Conflict Resolution 2, 1958.

Chapter 11

1. Yukl, Gary A. Leadership in Organizations. (London; Prentice-Hall International, 4th Ed., 1998).
2. Bass, Bernard M. Handbook of Leadership. (New York, NY; The Free Press, 1991).
3. MacGregor, D. The Human Side of Enterprise. (New York, NY; McGraw Hill, 1960).
4. Bass, Bernard M. Handbook of Leadership. (New York, NY; The Free Press, 1991).
5. Shaw, Marvin E. Group Dynamics. (New York, NY; 1981).

Chapter 12

1. Bass, Bernard M. Handbook of Leadership. (New York, NY; The Free Press, 1991).
2. Blake, R.R. and Mouton, J.S. The Managerial Grid. (Houston, TX; Gulf, 1964).
3. Bensimon, Estela and Robert Birnbaum, How Academic Leadership Works. (San Francisco, CA; Jossey - Bass, 1997).

Chapter 13

1. Bass, Bernard M. Handbook of Leadership. (New York, NY; The Free Press, 1991).
2. Bass, Bernard M. Handbook of Leadership. (New York, NY; The Free Press, 1991).

Chapter 15

1. Bass, Bernard M. Handbook of Leadership. (New York, NY; The Free Press, 1991).
2. Fiedler, F.E. A theory of leadership effectiveness. (New York, NY; McGraw-Hill, 1967).
3. Refer back to "Angle into the Current" on page Mark: insert page # after final draft is done.
4. Fiedler, F.E. A theory of leadership effectiveness. (New York, NY; McGraw-Hill, 1967).
5. Since the studies of French and Raven (D. Cartwright, ed., University of Michigan, 1959).
6. Bass, Bernard M. Handbook of Leadership. (New York, NY; The Free Press, 1991).
7. Blanchard, Kenneth H. Management of Organizational Behavior. Prentice-Hall, 1977.

Chapter 16

1. Burns, James MacGregor. Leadership. (New York, NY; Harper Torchbooks, 1978).
2. Burns, James MacGregor. Leadership. (New York, NY; Harper Torchbooks, 1978)...
3. Yukl, Gary A. Leadership in Organizations. (London; Prentice-Hall International, 4th Ed., 1998).
4. Yukl, Gary A. Leadership in Organizations. (London; Prentice-Hall International, 4th Ed., 1998).
5. Burns, John S. The Journal of Leadership Studies. "Defining Leadership: Can we see the forest for the trees?" Vol. 3, No. 2, 1996.
6. Tichy, Noel M. The Leadership Engine. (New York, NW; HarperBusiness, 1997).
7. Burns, James MacGregor. Leadership. (New York, NY; Harper Torchbooks, 1978).

Chapter 17

1. Burns, James MacGregor. Leadership. (New York, NY; Harper Torchbooks, 1978).
2. Koslowski and Doherty, "Integration of climate and leadership," Journal of Applied Psychology, vol. 74, 1989.
3. Schein, E. H. Organizational Culture and Leadership, (San Francisco, CA; Jossey-Bass, 1992).

Chapter 18

1. Fishbein, Martin & Ajzen, Isek. Belief, Attitude, Intention, and Behavior. Reading, MA; Addison Wesley, 1975).
2. Fishbein, Martin & Ajzen, Isek. Belief, Attitude, Intention, and Behavior. Reading, MA; Addison Wesley, 1975).
3. Fishbein, Martin & Ajzen, Isek. Belief, Attitude, Intention, and Behavior. Reading, MA; Addison Wesley, 1975).
4. Janis, I.L. Victims of Groupthink. (Boston, MA; Houghton and Mifflin, 1972).
5. Schlesinger, Arthur. A thousand Days, (Boston, MA; Houghton and Mifflin, 1965).
6. Schlesinger, Arthur. A thousand Days, (Boston, MA; Houghton and Mifflin, 1965).

Chapter 19

3. Fishbein, Martin & Ajzen, Isek. Belief, Attitude, Intention, and Behavior. Reading, MA; Addison Wesley, 1975).

About the Author

 ***William P. (Bill) Robinson*** assumed his duties as the 17th president of Whitworth College in Spokane, Washington, in July 1993. He came to Whitworth from Manchester College, in Indiana, where he served as president from 1986 to 1993. Like Whitworth, Manchester is a private, church-related liberal arts college noted for its academic excellence.

Since arriving at Whitworth, Bill has focused on expanding the college's financial resource base, overseeing capital projects, improving communication and organizational structure on campus, and opening up new lines of communication with alumni, friends, and other constituencies of the college.

Whitworth continues on a very promising trajectory under Bill's leadership. For the past five years, undergraduate enrollment has been at its capacity of 1,600, with total enrollment at more than 2,000. In addition, the college's academic profile and student retention numbers are at all-time highs. Whitworth has recently completed a number of capital projects, including its beautiful new campus center, a renovated science center, an athletics complex for soccer, softball and field events, and an expanded and refurbished classroom/faculty office building.

A communications scholar who has distinguished himself as a teacher and leader, Bill received his bachelor's degree from the University of Northern Iowa, his master's degree from Wheaton College, and his Ph.D. from the University of Pittsburgh. He also did postgraduate studies at Princeton Theological Seminary and the

Moody Bible Institute. His scholarly work focused on organizational, small-group, cross-cultural and interpersonal communication.

Bill is a founding co-chair of the Higher Education Leadership Group of Spokane and serves on the boards of Whitworth College, Princeton Theological Seminary, the Whitworth Foundation, the Washington Association of Independent Colleges and Universities, the Association of Presbyterian Colleges and Universities, the American Council on Education Presidents' Task Force on Teacher Education, the National Association of Independent Colleges and Universities, the Northwest Conference Presidents' Council, the Northern Life Insurance Educators Advisory Board, and the U.S. Bank, Spokane/North Central Washington Region. In addition, he serves as the immediate past chair of the Spokane Regional Chamber of Commerce Board of Directors.

Bill was born Sept. 30, 1949, in Elmhurst, Ill. His wife of 28 years, Bonnie, is a classical pianist and organist. The Robinsons have two daughters, Brenna and Bailley, ages 23 and 18, and a son, Benjamin, 21. Brenna is a Whitworth alumna (Class of 2000), and Ben is a member of the college's Class of 2003.

Whitworth students quickly become accustomed to seeing Bill among them, cheering at sporting events, enjoying plays and concerts on campus, visiting in dorm lounges, playing noontime hoops, and sharing meals and conversation in the dining hall. Both current students and alums mention how much they appreciate the fact that he knows them by name and obviously enjoys joking with them as well as discussing the big questions of life. In fact, Bill's connection with students is integral to his person and to his presidency. "My richest moments at Whitworth are the ones I share with students," he says. "My calling is to work with and for them. I love being in their midst."

Dr. Robinson's e-mail address is wrobinson@whitworth.edu